Friedrich Ludwig Zacharias Werner, Elizabeth Alicia Maria Lewis

The Templars in Cyprus

Dramatic Poem

Friedrich Ludwig Zacharias Werner, Elizabeth Alicia Maria Lewis

The Templars in Cyprus
Dramatic Poem

ISBN/EAN: 9783743331488

Manufactured in Europe, USA, Canada, Australia, Japa

Cover: Foto ©ninafisch / pixelio.de

Manufactured and distributed by brebook publishing software (www.brebook.com)

Friedrich Ludwig Zacharias Werner, Elizabeth Alicia Maria Lewis

The Templars in Cyprus

THE TEMPLARS IN CYPRUS

A DRAMATIC POEM

BY

FRIEDRICH LUDWIG ZACHARIAS WERNER.

TRANSLATED BY E. A. M. LEWIS.

"God has given the Increase."
1 *Cor.* iii. 6.

LONDON:
GEORGE BELL AND SONS, YORK STREET,
COVENT GARDEN.
1886.

Dedication

TO

HIS DEAR FRIENDS OF BOTH SEXES

BY THEIR FRIEND.

Tho tears are upward to God's throne ascending,
We wept beside the fount from five jets streaming;
All God sends down strives back to reach Him. O'er us
He lets seven stars pour forth their radiant gleaming,
Man's darkness to annul their lustre lending,
And light whereby to decorate the Torus.

But when the eyes of man
Can that which is for him alone discover,
Then Him that All is, he has comprehended.
Then tears and stars for him alike are ended;
Then is he God's; deceits and shams are over.
Meanwhile, let tears and stars, with scintillation,
Till those are dried, these set, maintain their station.
We, till the Lord's sign come, will pray with supplication.

Written on Mid-Lent Sunday, 1807.

In "The Templars in Cyprus" Werner ascribes to a Carmelite body, calling themselves "Sons of The Valley," the downfall of the Templar fraternity, designed with a view to the establishment of a more extended system of mysticism (which he calls the "Valley of Peace"); to make way for which the poem hints that the Templars are to be destroyed.

The activity of the "Valley" does not appear, except in the glimpses of it shown in the character of its two highly mystical delegates, ECHO and ASTRALIS, and an intimation of MOLAY's in the last Act that he has authority for what he is doing, and will account for his actions to the "Valley."

Werner was a Freemason, and his religious notions, of which he makes "SIR ROBERT" the mouthpiece, were, at the date of his writing this poem, of a theosophic order. In fact he aimed, at that time, at establishing a New Religion of his own invention; though ultimately he became a Priest, and preached in Roman Catholic pulpits.

PROLOGUE.

IN darkling night, mid wind and tempest's roar,
A light is shining from a burial-ground;
The furious storm, a moment, and no more,
Has quenched it, then it flares anew—each mound
Green-turfed it brightens which lay dim before,
And radiates all the azure ether round!
This is the aureole of that Order old,
Once for the Temple's guardianship enrolled.

Art has not drawn the curtains back that hide
The inner mysteries; we do but hear
The echo of the billows' distant tide;
But to no searching is the sea made clear.
Forth drawn from ancient night the world did glide;
Yet showed no working of the lever's gear!—
Historians still things seen and known declare;
The Undiscovered is the poet's share.

What I can show you is not much to tell,
If only outward forms we contemplate;
A group of men like many we know well,
Athirst for glory, over-borne by fate;
With eyes humane where pity's dewdrops swell,
Not independent heroes, worldly great!
They would not one should shine above his brother,
For every one is member of the other.

Yet draws it near to full perfection's goal,
This friendly calm where all self-seekings cease.
No stone predominates o'er the Building's whole,
And no blasphemer shames the old Order's peace.

Nailed to the Cross is every egoist soul,
Nor guerdon craves for martyr's services.
Only a bower of roses, far away,
Mist-veiled springs from the dust of green decay.

Then pause and contemplate the picture fair
Of times whose virtues are for ever gone ;
Bright fields Elysian are dispersed in air,
The infant from the mother's breast has flown,
His shield is bright with wisdom's chilling glare ;
But blind his inner eye is as a stone—
For darkness, tomb-like night, beclouds our way
When glows no more within the heavenly ray.

'Twas flickering faintly in the Templar band,—
They are but shadows of their old renown !
Taken from them is now the Holy Land.
World-wanderers are they scattered up and down ;
Only a pious few maintain their stand.
The Order's doomed beneath death's deepening frown,
Nor are they hostile hosts that deal the blow,
Their own unworthiness must lay them low.

At Philip's beck the gathering storms draw near,
With rolling thunders, but they will not mind.
E'en now the Vatican's fell fires burn clear,
And only Molay sees, the rest are blind.
Ah ! 'gainst their foes a bulwark they might rear,
Could they, degenerate ! needful courage find ;
They dare not—therefore now the engulphing wave
Must whelm them in fate's dark abysmal grave.

Now whilst they draw their faintest breath, their last,
Their strength already to the grave brought low,
Above them float the spirits of the past,
Like lightning flashes in dark night that show.
Still fain would some brave hearts the last die cast,
But, overborne, they like the rest must go,
For God the Temple Order called from strife,
That it through Death might be new-born to Life !

THE TEMPLARS IN CYPRUS.

And therefore still triumphant is the Pure,
Truth flourishes in funeral pyre's despite;
Her holy commonwealth, her reign is sure,
For out of smouldering ashes springs the light.
The flesh must severance from its frame endure
Ere the true body can be raised aright!—
Yet, till the grave's night passes, art shall show
To mortal eye the eternal covenant-bow.

PERSONS REPRESENTED.

EUDO, *formerly Marshal in the Crusading Army, now Adept Brother and Delegate.* ⎫
ASTRALIS (*called also* ASTRALON), *a fourteen-year-old Christian anchorite from the desert of the Thebaid in Egypt, Adoptive Daughter and Delegate.* ⎬ *Of the Valley.*

JAMES BERNARD MOLAY, *last Grand-Master of the Temple Order.* ⎫
The Presbyter of the Order.
PHILIP, *banished Duke of Anjou, Molay's confidant, now Serving-Brother and Brother of the Garden.*[1]
Marshal of the Order. ⎬ *Adept Temple Brothers.*
Draper of the Order.
Banner-Bearer of the Order.
CLAUS ROSNER, *a young German handicraftsman, and Associate of the Order.* ⎭

HUGO DE VILLARS, *formerly Grand-Commander, now Elder and Seneschal of the Order.* ⎫
The Preceptor of Cyprus.
HERIBERT, *Ex-Prior of Montfaucon.*
SIR NOFFO DI NOFFODEI, *an Italian Knight.*
SIR GOTTFRIED VON SALZA, *a German Knight.* ⎬ *Other Templars.*
SIR ROBERT OF HEREDON, *a Scotch Knight.*
SIR CHARLOT DE GUYONNE, *a French Knight.*
BROTHER SQUIN, *called* CYPRIANUS, *Chaplain of the Order, Molay's private Secretary.*
SERVING-BROTHER OTTO, *Bell-Ringer.*
SERVING-BROTHER GREGOR, *Molay's Attendant.* ⎭

FRANK OF BRIENNE. ⎫ *Young Secular*
ADALBERT, *Count of Anjou-Maine, Son of Philip.* ⎬ *Knights.*

A Tunisian Privateer.
A Troubadour.
WIFE OF CLAUS *with two Children.*
Four Preceptors
Knights, Chaplains, Serving-Brothers and Pursuivants of the Order, Workmen, Choristers, Tunisian Captives, People.

The scene is laid in the island of Cyprus, at Limasol. The action is in the year 1306, and occupies two entire days.

(Richard Cœur de Lion conquered Cyprus from Isaac Comnenus, brother of the Emperor Manuel, in 1191, and sold it to the Templars, who returned it to him in 1192, when he ceded it to Guy de Lusignan in indemnification of his claims to the kingdom of Jerusalem. The Templars reserved their Preceptory at Limasol, and the King fixed his residence at Nicosia.)

[1] So is called the Gardener of a Templar Lodge or Preceptory.

ACT I.

SCENE I.

Forecourt of the Templar-House; in the background the Church, to the right of which adjoins the yet unfinished building of the Society surrounded by scaffolding, to the left the Castle of the Order. Before the Church, the statue of the Risen Saviour with the flag of victory. Early morning. The bell sounds to matins.

Templars and people cross the stage, some coming out of the Church, and some going in. A Knight Templar and a Priest thus meet.

KNIGHT TEMPLAR.

PRAISE be to Jesus Christ!

PRIEST.
Eternally!
[They go together into the Church. ASTRA-
LIS *approaches, carrying a mendicant's bag, and dressed in bright yellow.*[1]

ASTRALIS (*Alone*).

Soon will the jubilant sun pour forth his rays,
The little bell of morning rings him greeting.—
Author of Life, I also give thee praise!
Soon, Robert, will thy feet, to forest fleeting,

---

[1] It was only in later times, and in the West, that the ecclesiastical Anchorite-garb became dark in colour. The early Christian Anchorites and Cenobites of the East, as in the Egyptian Thebaid and so forth, were brightly clad in yellow, blue, &c. &c.

Tread lightly o'er the flower-enamelled ways,
Plantains and palms to cool thy path competing.
Oh, cam'st thou soon!—The Master I will move
With prayers, who also won the Crown of Love!—
> [*She kneels in the background before the statue of the risen Prince of Victory.*
> [CLAUS, *with his wife* ANNE, *and other mechanics and labourers carrying various tools come forward.*

CLAUS.

Comrades, fall to! 'Tis morning bright! For shame,
Sluggards! Behold the Knights already wend
Home from God's service! Quick, fall to! We've now
But seven weeks to St. John, and for that feast
Must be complete the Sacristy. So wills
Great Molay, who knows work, and to reward it!

ALL.

Long live he!
> [*They mount the scaffolding and set to work with alacrity.*

CLAUS.
Now, bestir! Anne, bring the mortar!

ANNE.

There 'tis.

CLAUS.
How long I have carved this capital's
Embellishment, yet come not near the end!

AN APPRENTICE.
What then—one capital?

CLAUS.
Thou'd'st call it one.

APPRENTICE.
Were it indeed the dome itself!

CLAUS.
                    Oh, fool,
Each capital's a dome, for it supports
The vaulting of the roof which shuts it in.
Make thou thy pillars for the capitals;
The dome, forsooth, will follow of itself.

ANOTHER APPRENTICE.
Your speech is like our valorous lord's!

CLAUS.
                    May be,
Since seven long years I've served the noble Molay[1]
And am,—like all things here,—his handiwork.

ANNE.
Claus!

CLAUS.
Well?

ANNE.
        See there! the lancers newly come
From France, are being mustered!

CLAUS.
                    May be so!

ANNE.
Well-looking folk! So fair, so fresh, so agile!

A CHURL.
The Order's bought all that!

CLAUS.
            Bungler!—It may
Fair presence buy, not discipline and skill;
These it can only to exertion give.

---

[1] Molay was admitted into the Order about 1265, and had distinguished himself under the Grand-Mastership of Guillaume de Beaujeu.—*Trans.*

A WORKMAN.
Who would not be a soldier! Helm and lance!
How different from the apron and the trowel!

CLAUS.
Think'st so?

WORKMAN.
Aye sure!

CLAUS.
The noble Master Molay
So thinks not.

WORKMAN.
No?—and he a man of war!

CLAUS.
He says, before God's kingdom comes on earth,
Lances must plough-shares be and armour trowels!

SEVERAL LADS.
How?

CLAUS.
And the sword be changed into a plummet,
And it shall have two fastenings: Strength and Truth.

THE CHURL.
What may he mean?

CLAUS.
How should I tell thee, bungler?

[*During these remarks, they disperse, as they work, into the side-wings;* ANNE *also, who drags the mortar after her husband.*

ASTRALIS (*rising from prayer*).
O thou, the eternal Mother's gracious Son,

Thou beckon'st me towards love's thorny throne—
I love—my heart foretold!
> [*She remains standing, scarcely looking
> round. A troop of young soldiers
> of the Order come forward, singing.*

                  Adieu! Adieu!
O Fatherland, Mother, and Friends!
Adieu, thou beloved one weeping for us,
      We follow together
The banner that's cheerfully floating above,
The Cross that shines o'er us with love!

GOTTFRIED VON SALZA *comes forward.*

         A SOLDIER.
The knight!

      ASTRALIS (*in the background, Aside*).
    Yet Robert comes not!

    GOTTFRIED (*to the soldiers*). Are all here?
                          [*He inspects them.*

         ASTRALIS (*Aside*).
Doth sickness fold him in its close embrace?
Or lieth he e'en now transformed by death?—
I will but to the little door, and beg
Oblation for my daily need, then go.
> [*She goes to the little Temple door in the
> background, and rings, while she calls
> rather loudly—*

Praised be Horus![1]
         (*Aside.*) Still must I forget
How in this land they style the Valley's Master!
            [*Aloud in the doorway—*
Praised be JESUS CHRIST!

---

[1] Horus was the Rising Sun, and according to her teaching by the Sons of the Valley, one with the Risen Saviour, the eternal Fountain of Light.—*Trans.*

PORTER.
Eternally!
[*He hands her through the lattice a white loaf, which she puts into her satchel, then speaks softly with the* PORTER.

GOTTFRIED (*to the young soldiers whom he has continued reviewing*).
Swing rapidly the lances! Good! For so
The Master likes to see it.

SOLDIERS (*shouting gladly*).
The Master likes it!

[ROBERT *comes forward with javelin and hunting pouch, and a hound in leash.*

ASTRALIS (*hastens to meet him*).
Glad welcome, Paladin!

ROBERT.
Fair anchorite, thanks!

ASTRALIS.
Wilt thou again go hunting by the sea?

ROBERT.
Aye!

ASTRALIS.
Roses and acacias bloom again
On Isis,¹ Mary's image.

ROBERT.
Thou holy maid
Mysterious, strangely am I drawn to see
Thy Palms.

---

¹ Isis was mother of Horus.—*Trans.*

ASTRALIS.
And wilt thou taste the dates again?
Thou com'st? Thou wilt?—by morning's splendour lured?

ROBERT.
Lured by—(*suddenly restraining himself*). I come!

ASTRALIS.
And new-pressed wine I'll give thee!
[*Hastens off.*

GOTTFRIED (*newly conscious of* ROBERT'S *presence, goes up to him as he is going off*).
Whither so early?

ROBERT (*absently*).
Whither? (*Aside, looking after* ASTRALIS).
There she flits,
Fair dove of peace!

GOTTFRIED.
Off to the noble chase?

ROBERT.
For bear and boar. Come not within my throw!

GOTTFRIED.
You love to banter! But, do you not know,
To-day is Chapter held? You have the watch.

ROBERT.
I, say you? Has my turn so soon come round
To do that tedious office? They select
Another often, if one is not well;
Say I'm unwell!

GOTTFRIED.
You can do anything;
You are the favourite with the Master. You
Could very well—

ROBERT.
Yawn! (*turning round quickly to the soldiers*).
Now, my gallant lads,
Like you the service?

SOLDIER.
It but lacks its sauce,
An enemy's blood!

ROBERT.
Bravo!

GOTTFRIED.
Jesting apart,
Know you that the Tunisian, Christendom's
Worst foe, prepares, folk say, three privateers;
And one already cruizes in the bay?

ROBERT.
My friend, the Christian's nearest foe, the tiger,
That fourteen days has through the forest howled,
Demands our first attention. Two whole days
I've been upon his track.

GOTTFRIED.
You have not then
Heard all the news?

ROBERT.
When I can hear my horn,
And listen to the rushing of the storm,
What care I for the hiss of rumour's tongue?

GOTTFRIED.
Learn that the boat arrived from France yestre'en
Despatches of most grave importance brought,
And all with anxious expectation wait
The frigate that should anchor here to-day.

ROBERT.
With what?—May-be, from the Grand-Almoner

A letter with the glad and glorious news
Who carried at the Paris Candlemas
The first flambeau before our Lady; or else,
Tidings of comfort from the old driveller, Aix'
Grand-Prior, who tells how our good brothers sleep
Over the service of dear Christendom,
Now and for ever; and a host more such
Fine circumstantialities to be
In Chapter pompously read out to us.

GOTTFRIED.

You are a scoffer—But this time there's talk
Of serious import; for, as Charlot tells,
The Master yesterday the whole day long
Was with the Chaplain closeted, without
A taste of either meat or drink, dictating,
Hour after hour, long letters, which yestre'en
Went France-ward in the self-same ship that brought
Despatches hither; and 'tis whispered here
That his old friend the Cardinal has sent
Him intimation of most weighty matters,
Which are, 'tis said, in Paris set on foot,
And for the Order augur nothing good.

ROBERT.

They say! they whisper!—Augur nothing good!
Ah, shame upon you! Are you Knight or Priest?
Are we not men? and if we are, what harm
Can reach us from the puerile King Philip,
Backed by his host of sycophants and hirelings?

GOTTFRIED.

The Crown of France has been from olden time
Protector of our Order; and 'tis said
One friend offended's worse than seven foes.

ROBERT.

Old times are dead. Long sleeps in his cold grave
Our old antagonist Richard.—Side by side
The lion's heart sleeps soundly with the hare's,
Engulf'd in that insatiate monster's womb

That brings forth only to devour again.
What was, is now no more. Of venturous knights,
That pious handful, now Colossus grown,
Strikes terror to its nursing-mother Europe;
E'en he, the old man crafty, triple-crowned,
Shod in those sandals whose engirdling thongs
Bind all the world, dare not contend with us;
Else surely would he not from Interdict[1]
Have set us free for ever.

GOTTFRIED.
      True enough,
But were his wrath aroused against us?

ROBERT.
         Stuff!
Himself he armed us! And all else we lack
Can be supplied by virtue of that gold
Saved from lost Palestine, and dearly bought
With much brave blood and over-much lost honour.

GOTTFRIED.
Gold?—Ah! but what we need is arms!

ROBERT.
        E'en so,
And we shall find them easy to be bought
In these disabled, these impoverished times
When all is saleable. So we'll defy
The Lily and Tiara. Ah, believe!
The arrogance of Princes sprang from gold
And only gold can bridle it. With gold
They bind the servile hearts of human kind;
Spin stronger cords, and you shall wrench them free.
Metal is easily by metal ruled,
But by mind only can men's minds be schooled.

GOTTFRIED.
By our dear Lady, Robert, tell, I pray,

---

[1] The Pope had excommunicated the Order some time previously, but almost immediately withdrew the ban.—*Trans.*

Whence fish you all these maxims? in the woods
For ever coursing, yet you often talk
More wisely than that legend-worm, the Chaplain.

ROBERT.
These things, my friend, we hunt not out in woods
We surely shall in legends never find.
The spark of human reason glows as bright
In forests, growing with the cedar's growth,
As it is dulled within the narrow cell.
But your reminder of the sylvan joys
Comes in good time. Farewell!

GOTTFRIED.
       Saw you not yet
The Master? Sleeps he out the past day's trouble?

ROBERT.
He sleep!—Was ever such a stormy day
As could tire out the old man? E'en as I
Was starting out at three o'clock, he trod
That mountain-path already, which to climb
Before the sun-rise daily is his wont.

GOTTFRIED.
A quaint old grey-beard! Ever wise and staid
As fits his Masterhood—yet, when his heart
Is stirred to effervescence, forth he goes
At full burst over every obstacle.

ROBERT.
Poor heart, magnanimous, inscrutable!

GOTTFRIED.
There on the mountain, so the old folks say,
He with his tutelary spirit holds,
Each morning, converse; many indeed pretend
That, after heathen fashion—God be with us!
He doth the sun adore.

ROBERT.
  Knight-Brother, say,

Have you the great World-Spirit ever seen?

GOTTFRIED.
Never.

ROBERT.
Then question not to whom it is
The Master prays!—Come, deerhound, march! [*Is going.*

CHARLOT (*enters hurriedly*).
Know you
That Privateer of Tunis, which has cruised
Since yester-morning early in the roads,
Has anchored?

ROBERT.
Where?

CHARLOT.
Hard by the hermitage
That's on the strand.

ROBERT (*exclaims loudly*).
What there?

CHARLOT.
I'm sent to tell
The Master of it.

ROBERT (*to the soldiers*).
Comrades! are you fain
To earn your burgonets?

CHARLOT.
Would you then—

ROBERT (*as before*).
Come!

GOTTFRIED.
What! without orders and authority?

ROBERT (*pointing to his heart*).
They're here!
    [*To the soldiers, as he selects six out of the troop.*
    Come! thou—and thou—come also ye—
You seven brave fellows. Six. So we're full seven.
And were but seven valiant men so minded,
Methinks we should see no more privateers.

GOTTFRIED.
Whither away? 'Tis now lance exercise.

ROBERT.
That they shall learn in action! Comrades, forth!
For by mine oath, we'll seize the privateer!
    [*Hastens off with the six soldiers.*

GOTTFRIED (*calls after him*).
Do not forget the Chapter-watch!—He's gone,
O'er hill and valley!

CHARLOT.
    I must follow him
And warn him—(*hurries off.*)

GOTTFRIED.
    He's a foolish fellow, Robert,
And most peculiar!—If he speak twelve words
'Tis much to partly comprehend but five!—
Here comes the Chaplain.
    [GOTTFRIED, CHAPLAIN CYPRIANUS,[1] *coming out of the church—behind him a choir-boy.*

GOTTFRIED.
    Whither on your way
So early, reverend Sir?

[1] Otherwise, Squin de Florian, a native of Beziéres, who was brought before Philip the Fair and well rewarded, in return for an accusation on oath, charging the Templars with heresy, and with the commission of the most horrible crimes. See Addison, "Knights Templars," ch. ix.—*Trans.*

CHAPLAIN.
          I come from matins,
Pronounced is *missa est;* and we go home.

GOTTFRIED.
And have you on hand much business, reverend Father?

CHAPLAIN.
For Christendom's well-being, who would not toil?

GOTTFRIED.
True—in things temporal and eternal you
Are foremost! Yesterday, for instance, you
Were writing, so they tell me, all day long,
Most urgent and most weighty documents.

CHAPLAIN.
Wisdom and knowledge gave the Lord to me,
And these my gifts are often in demand.

GOTTFRIED.
Were not those missives to the Cardinal sent,
And to the Marshal of Brienne?

CHAPLAIN.
               To whom?—
I could not rightly say.

GOTTFRIED.
               But were they not
Dictated by the Master to yourself?

CHAPLAIN.
Dictated? Certainly, the phrases were;
But all the strokes and flourishes were mine.

GOTTFRIED.
They'd weighty matters in them; had they not?

CHAPLAIN.
To that I paid no very great regard,

But, if I rightly gathered anything,
The Order and the Clergy were concerned.

     GOTTFRIED.
Oh, Holy Father, tell!

     CHAPLAIN.
     I' faith 'tis all
I can recall to mind.

     GOTTFRIED.
    And yet you wrote it!

     CHAPLAIN.
Look you, good Gottfried mine! When one of us,
A Literate, writes, the letters buzz and swarm
By thousands in his head; he scarcely marks
What things are written by his crafty pen.
For instance: if "God greet you" be the words—
Two G's are writ, you think, as soon as spoke,
No, Gottfried, by no means: for each G must
Wind cunningly like spiral of a snail;
And this volute must also delicate be
As finest cobweb. In such subtle wise
The U must terminate, that should need be,
You might without much trouble call it X—
And only so the text can suit the reader;
It must be seemly even though it kill;
The writer,—well,—can always write again,—
And so provides himself, whate'er befall.
Is not this so?

     GOTTFRIED.
   Yes, that the mind can grasp—

     CHAPLAIN.
So grasp it then!

     GOTTFRIED.
     No easy thing, to
With all those crooks and twists!

CHAPLAIN.
                    Oh, friend, this art
Ranks o'er all other arts, the Quintessence
It is (as by my Prior I was taught
Who understood what I but speak) of all
States-craft and of all dogma.

GOTTFRIED.
                    I am lost
In wonder.
                CHAPLAIN.
            Yes, belovéd Son in Christ!
Therefore, observe! when high and noble Lords
Or Prelates shall be written for, one makes
Immense parade of twisted characters
Themselves unmeaning, and in context only
As they're together strung, to be explained,
And that in various ways as best they please;
And an assemblage of such crooked signs
(With which one wisely spares oneself the pains
Of what blind heathens call a "train of thought")
Is called, when it has neither stamp nor seal,
And if 'tis thick,—a book—an actual book, [1]
Such as the reader with his fists can grasp.
Per contra, when an aggregate of letters,
Meant to secure the writer his desire,
Has under it a pliant seal of wax,
And large,—'tis called an Instrument of Peace,
Bull, Mandate, Rescript, Record, Interdict,
Or when, as *reservatio mentalis*,
The wax is spared, and only L. S. stands
At bottom, then, d'you see, its value's nought.

GOTTFRIED.
That last I can most readily conceive.

---

[1] The word *book* is used frequently to imply a paper of political instructions or a signed agreement. See I. *Henry IV.*, Act iii., 1. "Our book's drawn: we'll but seal." Vol. I. Brewer's *Henry VIII.*, p. 234. Every composition whether play, ballad, or history, was called a *book*, on the registers of ancient publications.—*Chalmer's note to Henry IV.—Trans.*

CHAPLAIN.
Then mark! to writer of such documents
A fair caligraphy must be the sole
Object of his endeavours;—and the rest
He may entrust in faith to holy Luke,
The patron saint of painter and of scribe;
And prudent, whilst the letters form and flow,
Restrain his thoughts from dwelling on the sense.

GOTTFRIED.
Save that there is an ancient saw which says,
Men cannot choose but think of what they write.

CHAPLAIN.
Well, yes, my friend, with Laymen that may hold;
But then, the Church is, you should know, inspired!
The same, too, may be said of potentates,
And the superior Knights, so long as they
Believe, and pray, and offer to the Church.

GOTTFRIED.
Now see I clearly, Reverend Sir, how much
One learns by talking with the erudite!
And here's hot-headed Robert been to-day,
Boasting that in his forests he can learn
More wisdom far than you from breviary!

CHAPLAIN.
So says the heretic-dog, the ignorant dolt,
Who scarce knows how to scribble his own name?
And understands engrossing just as well
As I do Greek? (*Aside.*) But softly, Brother Cyprian.
(*Privately to the Choir-boy.*)
To Mother Elsie go, and bid her cook
The calf's-head for my luncheon, with sharp sauce.
[*Choir-boy runs off.*

GOTTFRIED.
Yet by the Master this wild huntsman's held
In great indulgence. Lately gave he him
A splendid charger.

CHAPLAIN.
                        Ah! that's like enough!
He has good points, poor Robert, though sometimes
He's indiscreet, but years will mend all that!
He comes not oft to Church, 'tis true, and that
Is bad! But then sometimes with meats and drink
He comforteth her servants—and indeed
Sent me quite recently a fine fat haunch.
And (mark the humour of it!) round the shank
He slung a silver collar, on it scrawled,
" Fellow to the fat Chaplain."

GOTTFRIED.
                        Bold, indeed!

CHAPLAIN.
It matters not, dear brother, for the Church
Only considereth the giver's heart;
And so a little cup I have had made
Out of the thick neck-band, and that fat haunch,
Devout, I ate to my soul's health, and gave
To Robert absolution for ten days.[1]

CHARLOT (*comes up*).
No devil could o'ertake Robert!

GOTTFRIED.
                        Let him go!

CHARLOT.
What recklessness!

GOTTFRIED.
            I'd not exchange with him!

CHARLOT.
Nor I, indeed! But I saw one to-day

---

[1] This Cyprianus, or Squin, is no bad portrait of the clergy of the early half of the fourteenth century. Worldly and vicious for the most part, indolent and inert, their wickedness was a powerful stimulus to the rise and spread of the German mysticism, and the pietists known amongst themselves as the "Friends of God."—*Trans.*

I'd gladly change with. He is a new Brother—
Doubtless you know of him already?

CHAPLAIN.
No,
Praise God, we know of nothing—

CHARLOT.
Then I'll tell you!
As yester-night, when from the bastion I
Was coming back, and to Colossa came;—
Chaplain! you know, just where the pretty hostess—

CHAPLAIN.
I?—God forbid!

CHARLOT.
Well, well, but hear me out!
As I rode up to the inn, a young esquire
Had just arrived before me. He is son
Of Poiton's seneschal, a rich old churl,
Who in his stronghold quietly consumes
The golden gain that in the holy wars
He plundered from the Turks. Good Sirs, 'tis long
Since such a head of game as this youth is
Has run into our snares! Just think of it!
He comes with ten Arabian steeds as rich
In gear as is our Lady of Malplaquet,
More handsome than the Master's own dear Tartar.
He has ten followers with him; strike me dead!
Why on the chapel altar the St. John
Is but an errand-boy compared with them;
So fine they are! Himself, a student lad
Of milk and blood complexion, so figged out,
So hung with chains and bells, that by their tinkle
He'd dance you on Shrove Tuesday the Chaconne
Without a fiddle.

CHAPLAIN.
Your preface end, and come
To facts.

CHARLOT.
       The fact's just this;—he has money which
Will soon, please God, melt in sweet Cyprus wine
For us, for he has withal the frankest heart
Of Brotherhood; this morning, quite unasked,
He bade them slip a flask into my wallet.

GOTTFRIED.
He comes to join the Order?

CHARLOT.
              Naturally!
He bared his heart to me, for we were both
Quite fresh and not fatigued, and we caroused
Into the night's small hours, and drank the healths
Of our brave brothers and our sisters fair.
Then in frank confidence he told me all.
His father, who from earliest youth had been
The Master's fellow-soldier, sends him now
His son to make a Templar, and he pays
More money for his woollen Cross than cost
A hundred gold ones.

CHAPLAIN.
          Knows the youth, in sooth,
His alphabet?

CHARLOT.
           Friend Chaplain, there's a lad
Who'll ask you posers. In one hour at Rheims
He argued with ten Doctors, and he laid
About him with such vigour, that like flies
His victims fell.

CHAPLAIN.
       That we may understand
No doubt, in sense of metaphor.

CHARLOT.
                    Ay, 'twas
To their skins metaphorical he gave

So dire a drubbing! How he carried on
With ladies, too, at the Burgundian court!
True, this he did not say, but then he gives
You all to understand.—A pretty lad,
Bedizened like a Sultan, young and rich,
And lively, irresistible! Watch well
Your Elsie, good friend Chaplain! for be sure
He'll track her out, more quickly e'en than I.

    CHAPLAIN.
Peace! miscreant! peace. This Judith slander not!

    CHARLOT.
Who holds her Holofernes' ponderous head
Lapped in her apron!—Come, let all be well!
Wash down your wrath in Cyprus wine with me!
Now must I to the Master bring report
Of the Tunisian pirate.

    CHAPLAIN.
     No, it shall
Not all be well! I excommunicate
You, trebly, miscreant!

    CHARLOT.
     Trebly, in return,
We'll crown you, Elsie and Poitou and I.

    CHAPLAIN.
I put you under ban!

    CHARLOT.
     But ban me not
From Elsie's paradise, is all I ask.

    GOTTFRIED.
Hush, Sirs! Behold what yonder, tottering, comes!

    CHARLOT.
Oh sorrow!—Here's the old head-shaker come!
    [*Commander Hugo, supported by a crutch,
     comes out of the Church.*

COMMANDER.
Why stand you there and gape like prattling women?
What? Have you nought to do?

GOTTFRIED.
We met by chance,
Just here, and one word led up to another.

COMMANDER.
Ay! there's no lack of words, that I know well.
But as for deeds! God mend it!—

GOTTFRIED.
Any way
There's Robert who does nothing. Even now
He strolls the forest careless with his hound.
There came—

CHARLOT (*quickly and aside to him*).
Hush, pray! Who'd be a tale-bearer?

COMMANDER.
Whst hast to do with Robert? Hast thou won
Like him three Horse-tails?[1] Hast thou put to flight
Five hundred Turks with fifty men, like him?
Yet he is too, a giddy-pate, God mend it!
On whom one must not leave the bridle loose.

GOTTFRIED.
What's more,—to-day's his turn at Chapter watch.

COMMANDER.
And goes to hunt, the scape-grace! Well, God mend it.
He knows the service; he will soon come back.

CHARLOT.
Most Valorous!

COMMANDER.
Well!—What sort of loom-product

[1] Turkish standards or ensigns.—*Trans.*

Have you got here of red and yellow silk
Upon your breast-cloth?'

     CHARLOT.
       'Tis the latest mode
At Court.

     COMMANDER.
  God!—Master Hugo!—These are they,
Whom thou didst band together to protect
Poor Christendom, and guard the Holy Land!
Behold this rabble, see how bare they are
Of honour and of discipline! To-day,
Is Chapter held, and one sets off to hunt,
One pranks himself with parti-hued Court bows,
Another goes to Church to gaze upon,
Instead of our Lord God, young wives and girls.
Alas! what proper knightly virtues these!
Here's Poverty, Obedience, Chastity,
Which you have all upon the Evangel sworn!
While sword-blades rust, the scabbards brightly gleam;
The Turk's proud crescent laughs to scorn the Cross;
Because 'tis only on the jerkins borne
Of such poor trifling creatures. Action's now
A dwarf, the tongue's a giant—Ancient Hugo,
Sleep!—Soon I follow thee!

¹ " What may our statutes, and how do our brethren observe them? They should wear no vain or worldly ornament, no crest upon their helmet, no gold upon stirrup or bridle-bit; yet who now go pranked out so proudly and so gaily, as the poor soldiers of the Temple?"—*Ivanhoe*, vol. iii., ch. v.—*Trans.*

² " Well thou knowest we were forbidden to receive those devout women, who at the beginning were associated as sisters of our Order, because, saith the forty-sixth chapter, the Ancient Enemy hath, by female society, withdrawn many from the right path to Paradise. Nay, in the last capital, being, as it were, the cope-stone which our blessed founder placed on the pure and undefiled doctrine which he had enjoined, we are prohibited from offering even to our sisters and our mothers the kiss of affection—*ut omnium mulierum fugiatur oscula*. I shame to speak—I shame to think of the corruptions which have rushed in upon us even like a flood. The souls of our pure founders, the spirits of Hugo de Payens and Godfrey de Saint Omer, and of the blessed Seven who first joined in dedicating their lives to the service of the Temple, are disturbed even in the enjoyment of Paradise itself."—*Ivanhoe*, vol. iii., ch. v.—*Trans.*

CHAPLAIN.
                    Ah, true indeed!
Sore is the need of Christendom!

                COMMANDER.
                            And you
Stand here and gape!

            CHAPLAIN (*offended*).
                Most Valorous—
                COMMANDER.
                            By your leave!
You too, Sir Cyprian, are not to my mind!
You are, I know, a learned man, for you
Can read and can engross; natheless that you,
An old Church-minister, should loiter here
With these young jackanapes, and gobble like
A turkey-cock, is scandal! Turn you to
Your breviary—and if you'd be so good,
Pray one or two *oremus* for myself.

                CHAPLAIN (*Aside*).
I'd rather far say masses for your soul,
Old croaking jay!—   [*Sneaks off with a malicious leer.*

    COMMANDER (*to* GOTTFRIED, *pointing to the soldiers*)
                Why stand these staring here?
Forth with them to the Place of Arms! Thou'lt find
A levy of new troopers just arrived,
Go practise them in thrusting with the lance;
There's work cut out for thee till Chapter time.
And lo! the horses too, not yet turned out!
The men not called to account! They're Templars just
Like thee!—Now go!   [*Exit* GOTTFRIED.

            COMMANDER (*to* CHARLOT).
                    And thou, my youngster, tell
What news thou bring'st us of the privateer?

                CHARLOT.
The Under-Marshal sends you word, the Turk
Has anchored fifty paces from the bastion—

COMMANDER.
God mend it !—And the Marshal calmly sits,
God mend it !—on the Bastion and looks on !
A Templar Knight !—How many Turks are they ?

CHARLOT.
Two hundred men, six Captains and a Colonel.

COMMANDER.
The barest handful ! Has the Under-Marshal
Essayed a brush with them ?

CHARLOT.
      He sends to beg
The Master and your Lordship, will despatch
In succour fifty men.

COMMANDER.
     The man's possessed !
Yet fifty men ! when on the Bastion stand
Already fifty ! That should be enough¹
For thrice two hundred Turks ! God mend it, but
That man's the merest milksop ! Pray, how much
Munition has he still ?

CHARLOT.
That I know not.

COMMANDER.
Here's a fine messenger ! Let be ! Let be !
I'll ask the old soldier who rode out with you,
For his old eyes have better sight than thine.
Thou'st been to tell the Master ?

CHARLOT.
      I was just—

COMMANDER.
Not with the Master yet ? And here he stands,

¹ " It used to be said of them: ' Un Templier poursuit mille Sarrasins,
deux mille, dix mille !"—Hist. de St. Louis, by the Marquis de Villeneuve.
— Trans.

God mend it, gossipping the last half-hour!
Not yet been to the Master? Does he know
The service, the obedience, or the rules?
March!—forth! Six minutes, and I come myself.
[CHARLOT *hastens away*.

COMMANDER.

These are the Temple's guardians! Ah, poor Molay!
Thou, thou remainest only! Yet with such
As these thou need'st must fall, and I! O, take
Me, Hugo! soon to thine eternal rest! [*Exit*.

SCENE II.

A natural garden set with many flowers and shrubs: Behind, a trellis adjoining a court-yard, and at the side, part of the Temple-court, with Farm-buildings.

PHILIP (*busy gardening, sings*).

Ere the early sun has left his bed,
(While yet from the steaming sea
Above and below floats the morning-red,
Nor with gleaming spear strides he;)
Hither and thither the blithe birds go,
Singing above and singing below
    A song, a jubilant song.

Little birds, why are ye always so gay,
As ye welcome the sun's warm fostering ray?
We rejoice that we live, and exist through the hours,
Rejoice that such blithesome companionship's ours.
Our fashion is good,
    So gaily to flit through the wood;
While fann'd by sweet breezy dawn's quickening powers,
    The sun too is merry of mood.

Little birds, why sit ye silent and pressed
To the eaves in your mossy nest?
We sit, for we feel not the warmth of the sun;
Night has buried his beams in the waves, every one;

But through the night
The sunray bright,
Reflection fair of the glad sunlight,
Faithfully shines through our dark, that we
May abide in a calm felicity.

Oh Youth, oh, soul, sweet morning-tide,
When we with hearts expanding wide,
Alert and awake in the spirit are,
Exulting in life's fresh pride,
Thou hast flown afar, afar.
We old men sit alone on our rest!
Only the lovely after-glow
Of youth's morning pride,
By the roseate dawn-flush glorified,
Our old age forsakes not that by it is blest;—
'Tis the calm of contentment thought-sanctified.

[*Leaves off singing.*

The song goes tingling through my aged nerves
Like hot-spiced wine. Delicious days of youth,
O, were ye endless!—But, who's this comes here,
So richly, so fantastically clad?
Perhaps a novice of the Order! Then
I'll in my usual fashion, test his worth.

[*Goes on busily digging.*

(*Enter* FRANK *of Puikra, dressed richly and rather fancifully as a dandy of the fourteenth century, but not outré. He wears peaked shoes, doublet and mantle bordered with bells.*)

FRANK.
Friend, can I with the chief of Templar Knights,
Grand-Master Bernard Molay, speak?

PHILIP (*without interrupting his work*).
                                        Perhaps.

FRANK.
Then say where I can find him.

PHILIP.
                    You can find

The way to him more easily by far,
Than, when once found, you can go back from him.

FRANK.

You speak in riddles.

PHILIP.
You're a walking riddle!
For by your pointed shoes with bells, forsooth!
And by your jingling doublet, who could tell
If you a sexton or a court-fool were!

FRANK.

You are a jester!—Show me to the Master.

PHILIP.
Look straight before you—past the Crucifix—
Along the wall—there through the trellis-door
A pigeon-house—you leave it on the left.
Now comes a brook—is't not so? A grey man
Is standing by it with a stable-bucket—
Now he draws water—that's the Master Molay!

FRANK.
That small thin man, who wears a trooper's jacket,
And like a groom a bucket holds? You jest!

PHILIP.
You mannikin, the man whom you call small
Is such a man that spite his sixty years
A dozen such light, child-men he could bear
To our dear Lady of the Mount, pick-back,
As lightly as he now fate's mill-stone bears.

FRANK.
Yet say why the Grand Master of the Order
Does servant's work?

PHILIP.
Nay, rather tell me why
You plant the cabbage by another hand,

Which yet you will with your own mouth consume?

FRANK.
Scarce know I, 'sooth, which I should most admire,
The Master there in aspect of a clown,
The clown with Master's tone and Doctor's sense!
I stand amazed.

PHILIP.
Stand not amazed—nor prate,
But act! I also must to work. Farewell,
Sir Wonder-struck! and have you not enough
Of food for wonder, ask the Master. See!
He comes himself! [*Goes.*]

FRANK (*Alone*).
A churlish fellow! yet
I cannot bear him grudge. Now nearer comes
The Master! How my heart beats! An old man!
Yet so impetuous—something in his look,
That well might make me humble, and withal
So mightily attracts me.

MOLAY (*in riding-doublet, a covered stable-bucket in his hand, comes up quickly, calling behind the scenes*).
Philip! Philip!
(*Becoming aware of* FRANK *as he comes on*).
Pardon! My sight deceived by distance, I
Mistook you for my gardener. What's your wish?

FRANK.
Are you indeed th' august Grand-Master Molay?

MOLAY.
My name is Molay. Well? Your business, friend.

FRANK.
I am the son of Henry of Brienne.

MOLAY.
The Seneschal of Poiton?

FRANK.
Even he.

MOLAY (*sets down the pail and hastens to* FRANK *with open arms*).
Ah! Welcome then a thousand, thousand times,
My heart's dear lad of gold! And tell me now
What does thy father? stumps he bravely yet
Upon that wooden leg?—

FRANK.
Yes, but three years,
He goes on crutches.

MOLAY.
Poor friend! Lives he still
His own old life? Doth he still polish up
The lances? Gives he drink to the Polak
And to his faithful Nimrod?

FRANK.
He is dead.

MOLAY.
Then let him pass!—Doth he still think of me?
Hath he not sent me greeting? Hath he not—— ?
Forgive! I'm well-nigh wildered with the joy
Of seeing mine old faithful Henry's son!

FRANK.
These words he sent you. "Brotherhood and Gaza."
And after them——

MOLAY.
Right, right! That was the watchword
Of our eternal bond of brotherhood!
Ah, Gaza, Gaza! Plague on my hot zeal!—
Has he had nought to tell you about Gaza?

FRANK.
A thousand times he has, and how he lost
His leg, in action sorely wounded there.

MOLAY.
Ah true! 'tis true!—but through whose fault was it?
I'll tell thee all!

FRANK.
If you would first permit—

MOLAY.
No—now it must be—for my heart will feel
More light when I've related to the son,
In its true colours, all I owe his father.
His wooden leg resulted from my rashness,
In the last holy war—quite forty years
Since then have flown already—we two served,
Beardless and bold, two lads of noble birth,
Under the brave Count Robert of Artois,
Who, too adventurous brother of St. Louis,
Left at Mansoura victory and his life.[1]
I should have gained already the Red Cross;
But it was far above my poor deserts.
Thy father, though not many years my senior,
Was far beyond me in a wise discretion;
He often warned me; yet I ever fought
Unheeding, in the thickest of the fray.—
My spirit burnt within me to set free
The Saviour's tomb, or find my own tomb there.
At Gaza,[2] once surrounded in a mêlée,
And at a distance from my company,
A Mameluke in the shoulder wounded me—
God ease his soul, he was a valiant blade!—
And stunned I fell to earth. But Henry saw,
And like a startled lion hewed his way
Through the throng'd Saracens. His black horse fell,
He fought on over me, tho seeming dead,

[1] His body was never found. Fellow-victims of his rashness, fell the Earl of Salisbury and other leaders, and 1,500 Templars, Hospitallers, and English; and this disaster was followed by the captivity of St. Louis and the surrender of Damietta, which he had taken at the commencement of the Crusades, by the aid of the Christian supremacy.—Trans.

[2] At the battle of Gaza, 312 knights and 324 serving brothers of the Temple are said to have fallen, as well as the Grand-Master Herman de Perigord.—Trans.

On foot.—Exhausted, then on his left knee
He sank, but on his right foot planted firm
He parried so the Heathen damascenes,
That, ere our succour reached us, they had fled—
But yet the javelin of a fleeing Turk
Struck his right knee-joint; then his nerveless arm
He tightened round my neck convulsively,
And in this fast embrace, and scarce alive,
They bore us to the camp. I opened first
Mine eyes, and, anguished by despair, beheld
My friend nigh unto death, who sacrificed
Himself for me. I nursed him carefully,
And when at last he woke—oh! more than I
Can tell thee was that moment's rapture!—Then
The sacred covenant on the Oriflamme,[1]
We swore to, and to seal it fast for ever,
Together were partakers of the Host
Which by the Patriarch's pious hands to us
Was with his blessing given; O! fresh morn
Of life, oh, golden dream! Come you no more?
Oh, come you never back?—Thou too, young man,
Must undergo the noontide's sultry heat.
Be like thy Father!—Say—doth he still love
To think upon our fighting days?

FRANK.
                                    His eye
Flashes youth's fire, when o'er the genial glass
He speaks of Molay and of Palestine.
And many more things tells he me on which
You purposely keep silent; how you saved
Him from the tiger's fury in the chase
And ever gave him booty that you won.
How when one day he fell into the sea
Near Damietta, you, without a thought
For your own safety, plunged in after him.
How you the Chan's head clave asunder, who—

---

[1] The consecrated standard of the Cross, which recurs so often in the annals of the Crusaders.

MOLAY.

Ah, let them rest, I pray, those boyish feats!
How kind my friend is still to think of deeds
That by myself have been so long forgot!
Yes, faithfully, brave soul, has he fulfilled
The vow of his young, scarce awakened heart;
He was my friend when I not yet could spell
The name of friendship. Many since have been
Comrades to me in war and victory;
But none of these my Henry!—

FRANK.

                      Confident
In this sworn covenant of his youth, he bids
Me bear to you this letter, with the prayer
That if convenient I may be received
Into the noble circle of the Knights,
Your brothers.¹

MOLAY.

            Ah! a letter? Let me read
Lines traced by that dear hand. Sit down the while.
But here's no stool—then seat thyself upon
This covered bucket! Stay though! my old steed
Of battle and the Tartar have not yet
Been watered, oft as they have suffered thirst
With me. Joy has eclipsed my constancy,
Which should not be. Do thou, my dear one, go
Down to that white and red house, 'tis the stall,
And there on the right hand they stand. Give drink
Freely to both! My usual morning-walk
Tends thither, but to-day my limbs are slack
With joy. Do me this kindness! in return
I'd give thy horse to drink!—

---

¹ Conformably to Rule LXII. "He who kindly desireth to give his own son, or his kinsman, to the military religion, let him bring him up till he arrives at an age when he can, with an armed hand, manfully root out the enemies of Christ from the Holy Land. Then, in accordance with our rule, let the father or the relation place him in the midst of the Brothers, and lay open his petition to them all. For it is better not to vow in childhood, lest afterward the grown man should foully fall away."
— *Trans.*

FRANK.
If you command.

MOLAY.
And come soon back again. [FRANK *takes the bucket and goes.*
What writes to me
My old companion in life's ups and downs? [*He reads.*
"Jack! greeting in God's name! Now here's my son.
Not bad, only—more knowing than his father,
A lady's man, a Doctor—brief—a fool!
Thou art a Man! Then make him one, like thee,
With or without the Cross.—Thy brother, Henry."—
There recognize I thee, frank rugged soul,
Rude as thy sword, word-chary yet how strong!
Ah! those disjointed times mere chatterers breed,
Not men like thee. So that's the sort of lad?—
With bell-hung doublet and pathetic tone!
Thou'rt right, mine ancient! First he must become
More simple—he must learn to comprehend
His nothingness, ere he be anything.
A Templar would he be?—Ay, trumpery
Enough goes with the Red Cross and to spare;
Yet is he son of Henry, of my friend!
So he must turn to good or to sheer naught.—
Lo, here he comes!—Now must fond memories
No longer sway me. Still, my heart! I am sorry;
But this while he must only see in me
The Master.

FRANK (*coming back.*)
Heartily the horses drink.
The Tartar has bespattered all my doublet.

MOLAY.
Ah! well! I crave forgiveness in his stead
And thank you for your trouble.—Sit down here
Upon the ground by me; my buffskin hose
Are well accustomed to it, and yours must learn.
[*Sits down on the ground.* FRANK *some-
what unwillingly does the same.*
Now look me in the eyes! for until now

I have not half regarded you—You are
A gallant youth. Your father's eyes—his hair
Of gold—Yet he was knit more closely—You
Some day, if my belief deceives me not,
Might rise to something great.

     FRANK.

        Your great soul sees
Me in the reflex light of its own greatness—

     MOLAY.

Ah! spare fine phrases, child! For no delight
Take I in greatness.—It is but to clash
And struggle for precedence, and usurp,
At last, the place that other men desire.
Are you yet bearded? Ha, short stubble only!
Yet, were you with the ladies cock o' the walk?—

     FRANK.

At any rate, the Countess of Provence
Has often given me vouchers of her favour.

     MOLAY.

For shame! Who asked for names? Have you perchance
Already tried your skill in feats of arms?

     FRANK.

At the Burgundian Court, from whence I come,
I've broken many a lance not without fame;
The Duke himself I hoisted from his saddle.

     MOLAY.

Your lords oft sit not tight!—Go on. Did you
By chance learn there some other things besides?

     FRANK.

The seven free arts and sciences at Rheims
I studied in the high school; and although
Nine times I there disputed, Fortune stood
My friend in these encounters also.

MOLAY. (*Springing up impatiently, whereupon* FRANK *also rises.*)
                                        Peace,
For heaven's sake, peace! For what could such a man
Learn more in all the world, what wish to learn,
When he knows everything? Say, my young friend,
What would you with our Order? You have been
By ladies much and highly favoured; here
Awaits you a cold vow of chastity.
You were a hero in the glittering tournée;
Here you will find no playful tilting-match,—
You wear a jingling doublet, tinkling shoes;
My old buffskin's my holiday attire.
The sharpness of your wit brought Doctors down;
We only deal death-blows to Saracens.
You are a master of all liberal arts;
And here the chief thing to be learnt is manhood!
Good sooth! go back to Rheims and to the Duke.
What would you here 'mid poor unlearned Templars?—

                    FRANK.
You make me blush with shame.

                    MOLAY.
                            That's something!

                    FRANK.
                                        You—
Forgive me—but you quite depress my spirit.

                    MOLAY.
If there's right stuff in it 'twill rise again!
But seriously!—What seek you in the Order?

                    FRANK.
Long since I've known that here were linked together
The flower of men in innocence' defence
And for protection of the Holy Land
And to safeguard the Right.

MOLAY.
                    So may, please God,
All valiant knights, e'en those without the Cross!

FRANK.
They are united in the practice of
Virtue, obedience and self-abnegation.

MOLAY.
So could not you do, in your modish doublet?

FRANK.
As you so closely press me, have I leave
To speak to you quite unreservedly?

MOLAY.
'Tis my desire.

FRANK.
            I am ceaselessly consumed
By thirst of knowledge. In the schools I learnt
High-sounding words, and, chain-wise linked together,
Conclusion on conclusion; but the truth
Hid in the kernel of those words, my search
Eluded ever—and still I vainly seek
To find the basis of the Infinite,
To gaze untrammelled on the naked Truth,
And contemplate her unveil'd countenance.
    MOLAY (*not ironical, but with suppressed emotion*).
'Twill come to pass!—Now let me hear the rest!

FRANK.
Oft have I heard your sapient Masters hold
That thing for which so ardently I strove,
And times unnumbered sought, but never found
But keep it hidden closely from the world,
That so the world burn not its fingers.

MOLAY.
                        What
Might that thing be?

FRANK.
          The true Philosopher's stone,
The key that opes the Future's iron door,
And all the hidden caverns of the Past
And Nature's most occult laboratory,
With revelation of her inner life.

MOLAY (*lost in thought over* FRANK'S *last words, after a little
    pause, with emotion, aside, as he looks upon* FRANK).
Poor child! For thee too has the Siren sung?
But, hold!—(*Aloud*)
                    You're seriously disordered, friend—
Such heated nervous ferment must, I know,
From manifold convulsions suffer, till
The hardening process gives it power to stand
Against life's frost, wherein no nature thrives
Except it be of cold and fungus kind.
Yet only surface-deep your ailment lies,
Thank God:—and, first of all, its remedy
In exercise and movement must be sought.
See you that man down yonder, standing by
The cabbage beds?

FRANK.
I see him, yes.

MOLAY.
                    He is
Philip, mine ancient gardener.

FRANK.
          Even now
I spoke with him. A sharp old fellow, though
He's somewhat rough, and not of the best manners.

MOLAY.
Polish his rudeness with your courtesy,
Whose mirror will thereby the brighter shine.—
See, how he toils,—how busily he digs
Assiduous to complete his daily task!—

Poor fellow! and there lacks him company.—
Go you and help him; few beds yet remain,
To-day, to-morrow, next day, all is finished.

FRANK.
Excuse me, if, with all submission, I
Remind you of my station—I, the son
Of Poitou's Seneschal—Peer of the realm!—

MOLAY.
We're all of us the sons of various fathers,
We've all been fain to sow before we reaped.
The Seneschal's father was a Marshal; his
Was Equerry, his, Falconer, and so on,
Back to the groom who currycombs the nags,
And on to the primeval Adam who,
Himself a labourer, needs must earn his bread
With sweat of brow. Then conversely perchance
May Philip's grandson wear a Cross of gold,
Whose grandson, in his turn, may rule as King
O'er land and people, and for frolic hunt
Some shepherd's sheep, himself once from a Peer
Of France descended.—So I pray thee, go
And help poor Philip!

FRANK.
I am still full tired.

MOLAY.
Stay not for that; your food will taste the better.

FRANK.
But in this knightly garb!

MOLAY.
              Oh, throw it off!
I must attend the Chapter—We shall meet,
At latest, at the midday meal.

FRANK.
And my
Reception?

MOLAY.
Learn to do and bear, the rest
Will work its own accomplishment. [*Exit.*

FRANK.
Is that
The foremost step to Wisdom, or the last?—
Alas! my head's already in a whirl. [*Exit thoughtfully.*

ACT II.

SCENE I.

Sea-shore, with a small Hermitage. In the background the Sea.

EUDO[1] (*Alone*).

THE stars move subject to their laws eternal;
  Harmonious all creation works, obeying,
By joys or terror ruled, one will supernal.
So also me shall one sole aim be swaying,
To which I woke through birth of blood and night;
Death's darkening shroud the bloody Cross must cover,
One day to wake to new existence bright,
Which now the silent Valley broodeth over!—
          (*Calling into the hut.*)
Astralis!—

          ASTRALIS (*coming out of the hut*).
Sir!—
          EUDO.
  The bread!—
          [*When she has given him the wheaten loaf which she received in the court of the Temple, and he has broken it into two halves.*

---

[1] Eudo, an emissary from the mysterious Order called "Sons of the Valley," is sent to prepare Molay for the fall of the Order. The "Sons of the Valley" had determined on their destruction because they revealed too much of the true light with which they had been entrusted, and sought openly to free mankind and defy princes, without the sanction of the "Valley."—*Trans.*

Take thou thy half,
And in thy dearest, love thou wholly God!—

[He gives to ASTRALIS *her half, which she eats gladly; as he brings the other half to his mouth, it becomes liquefied, and some of it dropping on his raiment, cleanses some spots that are on it. After he has consumed the remainder, he lies down and sleeps, for as long as is convenient to the economy of the piece. Whilst he sleeps,* ASTRALIS *busies herself in various ways, plants flower-shoots, and when these have grown up* [1] *she talks to them in their language, and sprinkles the flowers with the waves that come lapping around her, picks them, crowns with them the figure of Isis—or Mary—that is within the hut, and so forth: then* EUDO *awakes.*

EUDO.

Hast offered sacrifice?

ASTRALIS.
Prepared it only.

EUDO.

Hast prayed?

ASTRALIS.
Yes!—Ardently for Robert![2]

EUDO.
Sweet
The prayer! 'Tis the last time he comes to thee

[1] The above phenomena would, no doubt, be intelligible to the Theosophists. The "Valley" claims to be in possession of absolute truth, and of miraculous powers.—*Trans.*

[2] To Astralis, a deputy of the "Valley," was given the task of preparing Robert for the fall of the Order, and the establishment of a new Order, to be founded by him in Scotland.—*Trans.*

In gladness—Anguish waits on him, till ye
Shall in the Valley's peace united be!

ASTRALIS.
Alas! must death so soon engulph him?

EUDO.
                              Nay!
He must be purified to form anew,
With thee, a country for the Bounteous One!
Come, Sister, tender me the kiss of peace!
        [*After she has kissed the drops which had
            fallen on his raiment from the
            oblation of bread.*
Now—list!—
                ASTRALIS.
            So glad I feel, yet fearful! e'en
As heretofore when that first time, a child
High Isis' grot I entered.

EUDO.
            Time conceives
In fear and trembling, now, that which at last
It shall bring forth with joy. How oft hast thou
Beheld the Acacia's bloom since thou remember'st?

ASTRALIS.
Ten times at least.

EUDO.
            Full fourteen times it has
Attained perfection, withered, and decayed,
Since Isis newly formed thy spirit, and this
Soft tender covering lent it. Who revealed
To thee the Eternal Mother's presence?

ASTRALIS.
                              Thou!

EUDO.
Who let thee see the elemental war,
And how one breath of love can still it?

ASTRALIS.
                    Thou!

EUDO.
And him the all beauteous youth, our Master who
Rides on star-crowned, upon the beam of morn,
And flies the red-blood banner of the Cross,
Who showed him to thee?

ASTRALIS.
                    Thou!—and thou hast shown
My Brethren to me, in the Valley calm
Where lion roars not, and tears never flow.

EUDO.
Then must thou cheerfully their work fulfil.
Six days ago in Carmel's vale I sought thee,
Where Sharon's roses pour their perfume still,
And here where earthly storms still rage I brought thee
That now this youth thy heart should fire and fill
With love with which, foredoomed, thy fate has fraught thee.
Thou lov'st, he yearns to thee, but torn asunder,
His course must be where life's wild surges thunder.

ASTRALIS.
O Brother, mercy!

EUDO.
            Stay me not, but hear!—
The Templar league should wrestle self-forgetting,
But wantons idly, and unmasks the light;
For this its death-knell sounds, its sun is setting.
Who fails in force of will and vigorous might,
Him fate's dark storm whirls on, no hindrance letting;
The Templar league must pass away in sorrow,
And even Molay find through death new morrow.

ASTRALIS.
Even Molay?—

EUDO.
    To prepare for this the Master,

The Valley's brethren sent me to this land;
Thou must inspire, drive on bold Robert,—faster
And faster round him wind love's silken band;
Seize from the times' uprooting and disaster
The Master's staff for his beloved hand.
This task is thine, thus hath the Valley spoken.—
He comes,—be strong, thy vow must not be broken. [*Exit.*

ASTRALIS (*alone*).
ISIS, great Mother, high-favoured of God,
Thou that bathest all being in radiance divine,
  The Pitiful, Thou, the Eternal,
Approaching as Virgin to sin-stricken man,
That glorified, strengthen'd by infinite might,
  The Master, the Saviour hast borne!
Oh, HORUS, my Master,
If ever thou'st flamed on me from the red day-dawn,
If, oh ISIS, thou'st beamed on me from the tide's mirror,
  Give strength to me, feeble, for this mighty work!—
Enough to do for him, who mine is,
Accepting me through him, who mine is,
To exult with him, in Him who all is,—
By beauty subduing the strong son of power!
          [ROBERT *and six soldiers come up.*

ROBERT (*to* ASTRALIS).
Well met, fair anchorite maiden!
          (*To the soldiers.*)
              Ye'll haste up yonder rising,
And should ye see the Turks appear, signal for mine
  apprising.   [*The soldiers go.*

ASTRALIS.
Thou'st respite got from fighting. I'll let thine hair go free.
          [*She takes his helmet off.*

ROBERT.
What art thou, wondrous Being?

ASTRALIS.
          A fire-altar for thee!

E

ROBERT.
Oh, ever since these seven mornings past when first I found
   thee,
A spell of sweetest sorrow from thy beaming eyes hath
   bound me;
The breath of life that vibrates from the welkin and the
   wold
I draw but from thy lips, yet thou remain'st austere and
   cold!

ASTRALIS.
See'st thou yon goodly palm-blossoms, so tenderly inter-
   lacing?
Fain would they mingle their perfume and tints in a fervent
   embracing,
         Yet separate and cold,
         Each its station must hold!
They may not enjoy, they are only for blooming and
   gracing!

ROBERT.
Ha—   [*Suddenly sunk in thought.*

ASTRALIS.
   I was nigh forgetting!
         [*Bringing wine and fruits from the hut,
         and setting them before him.*
         See dates and cool palm-wine!

ROBERT.
To bloom—but not enjoy!

ASTRALIS (*childlike*).
         Ah, thou must not repine!

ROBERT.
And should I then think shame because this fire is in me
   burning?

ASTRALIS (*putting her arms round him*).
Gives not new splendour to the sky the roseate dawn's
   returning?

Pure shines the Virgin Mother, yet she lavishes her light!

ROBERT.
Art thou a Christian maiden?

ASTRALIS (*emphatically*).
Art thou a Templar Knight?

ROBERT.
(*Freeing himself with violence from her enciroling arms.*)
Ha! thou awak'st me from slumber, I'll loyally stand to
  my vow,
I'll flee thee, Enchantress!—

ASTRALIS.
Thou'lt flee?—Into Nature's kind bosom wilt thou?

THE SOLDIERS (*hurriedly running in*).
The Turks, knight!—

ROBERT.
Then follow, exultant, me into the thick of the fight!
  [*Hurries off with the soldiers.*

ASTRALIS (*Hastening after him with outstretched arms*).

Stay, Robert!—

EUDO.
(*Coming out of the hut, stern and commanding.*)
Astralis!

ASTRALIS (*suddenly pausing*).
Him draws, as it draws me, omnipotent Might,
Into blood, into night!   [*Goes slowly into the hut.*

EUDO (*Alone, with folded hands*).
So the lover retireth, but—Love
Waits the Light.
  [*Exit, on the same side as* ROBERT.

SCENE II.

Temple Garden.

PHILIP (*occupied throughout the scene with garden-work*).
FRANK (*in his previous costume, but without
mantle, working also*).

PHILIP.
Now, how do you like the work, young gentleman?

FRANK.
Right well—Yet see I not with what design
I have been set to do a servant's work.

PHILIP.
Design?—Why, look on these poor beans! They hang
Their heads as droopingly as though they strove
With throes maternal.—Loiter not, give water,
So drink they breath of life.—This water-melon
Is almost stifled in its leafy shroud.
I give it air—and see! as though it thanked,
It looks at me, confiding, from its leaves—

FRANK (*smiling*).
It looks at you?

PHILIP.
Its Master am I not?—
[*Keeps on working, now here, now there.*
The flaunting Ivy!—round the Vine-stock twined
So unabashed, its dark shade smothers up
The vine's best sap!—I bend it.

FRANK.
Somewhat rudely!

PHILIP.
Ah well! its leaves so glossy and so green
Indemnify me not for sweet ripe grapes.
Back, proud intruder! Thou, behind, may'st serve
To some good use, but my delicious fruits
Thou must not curtain, overweening one!
Pride take I also in my lowlier crop
Of roots,—my Endive, Sage, and Watercress!
Not brilliant they, but gracious gifts of God;
They heal and freshen our disordered blood.
Here it's too crowded. 'Tis the mass of Tulips;
They vaunt themselves as though the whole parterre
Were kept for them alone!—Out, out, vain things!
[*Weeds them out.*

FRANK.
O, pity for the splendid Tulips!

PHILIP.
　　　　　　What?
Because they blow so beautifully, should
My pious, poor herb-folk lie perishing?
Out with the trash! Why were ye not discreet
Enough to leave a little ground for others?
Ye give up nothing, therefore ye lose all.
　　　　　[*Going to another part of the garden.*
How now, thou sapless Cedar! stand'st thou yet?
I thought thou must have withered long ago,
Drained as thou art of vital power and sap.

FRANK.
Gardener! you'll be considerate, you'll not fell
This most majestic tree?

PHILIP.
　　　　　　Yes, he must go,
To-morrow, hence—This perishing intruder
Has lost himself amid the stir of life,
And robs the soil of its best juices.

FRANK.
                    'Tis
So old a tree!

PHILIP.
                    The rather, that it is!
An ancient evil must with all dispatch
Be abrogated—See, 'tis dead below,
And thinks, poor fool, that it shall live for ever,
With the whole garden for its sole domain.

FRANK.
Yet, grubbing up its roots you must destroy
The Larkspur too, the Chickweed, and the Mushroom,
And golden Wall-flower so rich of hue!

PHILIP.
Ah, that's but painted dust!—Quite long enough
Has all that rubbish from the thirsting Rose
Absorbed our Lord God's dew!—Ye noxious weeds!
The dew befits the Rose!—Away with you!
                    [*Roots out all the weeds.*

FRANK.
Be not too hot!

PHILIP.
                    Nay! better hot than lukewarm!

FRANK.
Saintfoin you cultivate, and Clover too?

PHILIP.
A German gardener brought it here; 'tis good
For fodder, so long-suffering too, it lets
Itself be five times mown without complaint,
And greatly prides itself if a sixth time
It brings to market its last remnant small
Of vigour, just that my old ass may eat.—
'Tis verily an excellent good crop!
But has one serious fault; it sucks its plot

So clean, that not one particle of strength
The soil retains—in three or four years grows
Not e'en the smallest Violet on such ground,
Far less a Vine or Rose. 'Tis useful now,
So it must stand; though gladly would I have
Some little space for Pinks and Mignonette.
For—is't not so, young Lord?—when you have filled
Your belly, eye and nose assert themselves,
And each demands its own especial share.
Aye, oft indeed I think, if our Lord God
Should take our stomachs, and should only leave
Our nose for scent, and our small pair of eyes,
That so we only lived by Sight and Smell,
We should be much less gross—much more alert.
Now many a man has got no nose at all;
That's the worse part of it!—You wipe your brow,
Your doublet you unloose.—Are you so warm
From such a little digging? (*Aside.*) Doth it work?

FRANK (*Aside*).
No, this I cannot stand, he drives me wild.
(*Aloud.*) Hark thee, old man, say truly, who art thou?
A peasant? Nay, most surely not! A Sage?
Perhaps my Genius, whose behest it is
To loose my shackles.

PHILIP.
   You are weary. Rest
Beneath this palm-tree's shade. Perhaps its leaves
Will tell you something, as at times they do.
It sounds more pleasant so than when another
Accosts you with such wares.

FRANK.
   But who are you?

PHILIP.
I? I'm a man.—And you?—Ah, yes!—the son
O' the Seneschal of Poitou!
  (FRANK *goes away*—PHILIP *looks after him.*)
   This youth will mend,

But hardly has the makings of a man,
A hero of humanity!—Alas!
Fate's hand alone can shape us into that;
But mostly grips us with such iron grasp,
That we lie shattered ere she has moulded us—
My Adelbert!—
    (*He stands deep in thought*).

   MOLAY (*comes up. He is in complete vestments*).
    So sad, belovèd Anjou?

      PHILIP.
Let me not hear again that tragic name!
Com'st thou from Chapter?

      MOLAY.
      Even now.

      PHILIP.
         Thou art
In strong excitement. What has passed?

      MOLAY.
         Oh, first,
Let me inhale God's air!

      PHILIP.
      My friend!

      MOLAY.
         Thou know'st
The long suppressed hostility with which
Philip of France eyes evilly our Order.
Only too gladly, lay it in his power,
He'd plunder us, and our possessions add
To those extorted, which nefariously
He grinds out from his burghers' bloody sweat.

      PHILIP.
I know him well, the kingly usurer!

MOLAY.

The crafty¹ Bernard Got, his bosom friend,
With whom he chaffered the Tiara for
Such paltry pay, is firmly leagued with him;
Our treasure, it may be, the ransom is
He promises to pay for Peter's keys.

PHILIP.

Tis very like him, priestly hypocrite!

MOLAY.

The Pope is at Poictiers, and even now,
So sends us word my friend the Cardinal
Præneste, there's a letter on its way,
Whereby the Master of the Hospital
And I are thither summoned with intent,
To organise, they say, a new Crusade.
The packet-boat of yesterday brought me
Præneste's letter, and the Brief may come
Perhaps to-morrow with the frigate.—You
Perceive the insidious snare!

PHILIP.
Aye, from the cowl
The devil's face looks out full evident!
This was the motive then that caused to-day's
Assembling of the Chapter?²

MOLAY.
This it was;
For there was urged to-day the weighty question,

¹ Bertrand du Got, a Gascon, Bishop of Comminges, Archbishop of Bordeaux, and Pope Clement V., who was the first Pope at Avignon, the Papacy having been transplanted thither under the auspices of Philippe le Bel. The chronicler Jean Villain said that the King and future Pope met privately in an Abbey in the depths of a wood near St. Jean-d'Angely, and then sold and bought the Papacy in a contract of six articles, sworn to on the Host. One of these articles involved the destruction of the Templars. Of the ten Cardinals created at his consecration nine were Frenchmen, a proof how he was the French King's creature.—*Trans.*

² Grand-Master (*loq.*): "It is not defect of power in us which hath occasioned the assembling of the congregation; for, however unworthy in our person, yet to us is committed, with this baton, full power to judge and try all that regards the weal of this our Holy Order. Had y

Should we, as cited by the Holy Father,
Compliantly betake us to Poictiers,
And there, before St. Peter's huckster'd chair,
Ourselves unarmed, surrender to the toils
By Philip cunningly prepared for us;
Or should we, at this crisis, publicly,
Anathemas defying, and the banner
Borne by the people's tyrant,—drop the mask,
And storm by their own soldiers' venal hands
The stronghold we have long since undermined
In secret, seeing it militates against
The pious pilgrim-folk, in whose defence
We're Templar Knights.

      PHILIP.
    Deep problem! Raged there storm?

      MOLAY.
Aye! So that in the whole long period I
Have served the Order, never have I seen
The like.

      PHILIP.
   Thy verdict was—

      MOLAY.
       For resolute,
Unflinching manhood in the cause of right,
For the plain duty of the present hour,
For open war with clergy and with crown.

      PHILIP.
And was—

St. Bernard, in the rule of our knightly and religious profession, hath said in the fifty-ninth capital that he would not that brethren be called together in council, save at the will and command of the Master, leaving it free to us, as to those more worthy fathers who have preceded us in this our office, to judge, as well of the occasion as of the time and place in which a Chapter of the whole Order, or of any part thereof, may be convoked. Also, in all such Chapters, it is our duty to hear the advice of our brethren, and to proceed according to our own pleasure."—*Ivanhoe*, vol. viii., ch. vii.—*Trans.*

MOLAY.
Outvoted!—

PHILIP (*embracing him*).
Rest on thy friend's heart!

MOLAY.
Brother, thou know'st if I mean loyally,—
How warmly for my brethren's welfare beats
My heart, wear they the Cross or wear it not,—
Too warmly beats!

PHILIP.
Alas! yes!—Let it beat!—

MOLAY.
Thou know'st in how degenerate a case
I found the Order, from those rabble dregs
How much I have created, how much more
I fain would yet create!

PHILIP.
And it shall be
Created!
MOLAY.
No—'twill not be! Nevermore!
From such a lifeless mass the Phœnix pure
Will never rise!—That they should misconceive,
That they should scorn me, that they should ignore,—
Nor even deign to dream of,—all that I
(Bear with my storm-tossed heart!) as sacrifice
Have freely offered in our holy cause,—
God is my witness, that I can endure!
But that they now, in the full light of day,
Blindfold their eyes, and cannot, will not, see
The one thing needful to humanity
For whose defence they're consecrated; this
Torments me with a thousand martyrdoms.

PHILIP.
Thou livest still—thou art a young man still!

MOLAY.
In contact with their icy callousness
My warm life freezes. Philip! Friend!—I feel
Now, after sixty long years' faithful fight,
That I have lived in vain!

PHILIP.
Despair not yet!—
The king's sword has not power to overthrow
Your sovereign league!

MOLAY.
Ah! not the king I fear;
Not through the king the Order falls, but through
Itself, and strangled by its sons. To shield
Their own most precious selves from chilling blasts,
They sacrifice the welfare of mankind.
Oh, bitter, bitter!—Must my Henry's arm
Have rescued me to live for times like these!

PHILIP.
Surely the Grand Commander, he was staunch
To stand by thee?

MOLAY.
Well, yes, he was; but yet
Thou know'st thyself how much the ancient forms
In which his spirit has been welded, now
These eighty years, have weight with the old man.
How break through these himself, so suddenly?—
In truth, his better spirit has been long
Enlarged, but prejudice constrains his will.
Should the whole Order, Christendom itself,
In ruin fall, he'd lay his life down; yet
The nobleman, the vassal of the Crown,
He cannot sacrifice. His reason shows
How void is the hereditary claim,
But though he sees, his shuddering will recoils.

PHILIP.
And Norfolk,[1] Armagnac and Villa Franca?

---

[1] Werner thinks only of the history of the *Order*, and his characters are for the most part typical rather than historical. There could have been no Earl of Norfolk present at the Chapter, because Roger Bigod,

MOLAY.
Thou know'st that haughty man, who more esteems
The golden dragon than the Stigmata.—
His verdict is, we should of England crave
Forgiveness that so many a time we stood
Across the path of lion-hearted Richard,
And were so backward his footstool to be.—
This done, she possibly might condescend
To pity our distress.

PHILIP.
And Armagnac?

MOLAY.
Expects some speedy miracle will save
The Church from losing her defenders.

PHILIP.
Aye!
Such is their way. Heaven must bestir itself
In lieu of them; and they'll look on.—The Roman
Gobbo, was he, too, mindful of the soil
That bred him?

MOLAY.
Quite!—To Poictiers he would go
Himself, and ask the Pope for Peter's sword:
"Then" cried he, "not our direst enemy
Could harm us."

PHILIP.
Rome, are these thy sons! O Brutus!
O Cassius!—and the others!

MOLAY,
Most of them

fifth earl, and last earl bearing that name, was twice married, and could
not have been a Knight Templar. He surrendered his earldom and
estates to Edward I. for a pension in 1302, with the proviso that they
would be returned to him should an heir yet be born to him. He died
childless in 1307, and his brother John inherited neither title nor estates.
Thomas Plantagenet, son of Edward I. by Margaret of France, was
created Earl of Norfolk in 1312, with possession of all Roger Bigod's
titles and estates.—*Trans.*

Are but loud-throated echoes ; they believe
No brand consumes the building's lower floor,
Although the roof be smoking. But the few,
Who see the flame, examine only how
Each, circumspect, may snatch his own small cell
Forth from the burning !—Then the rest may crash
Together, if so be God's will—Aye many
Whose boast is foresight, would not shrink to see
Substructure, dwelling-house, to ruins fall
If yet the gothic tower, with foliaged scrolls
And shining pinnacles could hang intact,
Suspended in the air !—

      Philip.
        Was no one, then
A man ?
        Molay.
   O yes !—twelve recently received
Would fain equip this very night the sloop,
And with a hundred soldiers sail to Rome,
London, Madrid, where not ? There help demand
From Princes, and, dare any of them refuse it,
Slay him forthwith. They dreamt they felt themselves
Appointed the sole saviours of our league.

      Philip.
Fools, fools !—for how can boldness profit us,
With immaturity ? Some night-sortie
Is planned with care, and straight with trumpet-call
They wake the enemy that he may see
The moon reflected from their shining helms.
Then whilst, scarce wak'd, he arms him for defence,
They, prudent, wheel their steeds about for fear
Their saddles might be sprinkled with some blood.
O gag your mouths, and task, instead, your hearts
And arms, ye rabble rout of parrots !—O Friend !
Your great full heart has lost indeed its way
Amid these desolate steppes !

      Molay.
       Such is my fate !—

'Tis for posterity to judge of me,
The Order has condemned itself to death;
'Twas my desire to save it, failing that,
My duty calls on me to share its grave.

      PHILIP.
What dost thou purpose then?

      MOLAY.
        With spirit pure
And manly heart, to follow my star's lead.—
A second letter from the Cardinal
I look for, with the frigate that should bring
The Brief. Should Philip show himself, declared,
The antagonist of the Order, then will I
To-morrow start for Paris;—fearlessly
Approach his throne-steps, and such truths proclaim
As many a long day since he has not heard
From his smooth sycophants. Then to the Pope
At Poictiers go, and all the subtle web
Of treacherous artifice unfold to him.
Avails that not, I'll whisper in his ear
How shameful were the means by which from France
He bargained the tiara. There's no means
So apt to overcome malignity
As showing that its secret game is known.

      PHILIP.
Reflect how great the danger, O my friend!

      MOLAY.
The *Order* hath reflected—I am he
That serves it, not its ruler. If denial
Beseems its youngest Knight—how much the Master?

      PHILIP.
Thy life—
    MOLAY.
    A loan is, which I must repay
With interest to the giver. I have gained
Therefrom a sum of precious hours, thank God!

PHILIP.
If thou should'st lose the game—

MOLAY.
                        'Tis never lost
When born of faith and courage.   Whether I
Be called to play the game out, or another,
Is matter of no moment.

PHILIP.
                        Yet bethink thee!
While yet it stands within thy choice.

MOLAY.
                        Say, friend!
If with the high I may the low compare,
Stood it not also in the Martyr's choice,
Not to have suffered for the truth he own'd?
Uncertain is the strife, but our defeat
Not yet assured.   Still fairly may I hope
To see perfidiousness succumb before
Our righteous cause.   The Order's holy rule,
My silver'd head, my very linen mantle,[1]—
The purple's brother—safely guards my breast
From every thunder-bolt.   E'en should it strike,
It cannot rob me of my firm belief
The seed my labour sowed will fructify!—
Thrice blest who falls a willing sacrifice
In duty's cause!—Yet
        [*His head, hitherto erect, droops, and he folds his hands.*
                        Might I reach my goal!—

PHILIP.
The goal of labour?   Dost thou yet believe
In that?—Deluded man!   see yon small snake,
So iris-hued!—With upward darts and shoots,
She seems to aim at reaching the high sun;
Poor fool, she sees a fluttering in the blue,

---

[1] The white mantle of the Templars was a regular monastic habit, having the red cross on the left breast; it was worn over armour, and could be looped up in battle.—*Trans.*

So dreams that she has wings. Yet can she fly?—
She can but coil in circles, nothing more!—

MOLAY.
Fie! from thy spirit no such emblem sprang!

PHILIP.
It came not with my spirit to this world;
Men wrote it there in characters of blood.

MOLAY.
And would'st thou blame the firmament, because
'Tis mirror'd turbidly in turbid eyes?

FRANK (*with bleeding hand, running in*).
(*To* PHILIP.) Water! old fellow! (*Perceiving* MOLAY.)
Pardon, noble Sir!

PHILIP.
What ails you, then?

FRANK.
I lay immersed in thought
Reposing 'neath the shadow of yon tree,
When near me drew a confident gazelle,
Lured by the fragrance of the juicy crops.

MOLAY.
My little favourite!

PHILIP.
Well?—

FRANK.
Some evil star
Next sent a jackal, nowise of the smallest.
He, furious, seized the tremulous beast, and rent
My heart with pity, and I uprose in wrath,
And ere he could destroy the gentle thing
I struck him, being unarmed, with my bare fist,
A blow that told. The slayer I destroyed,
And saved the victim,—and that's all.

PHILIP.
                              Destroy,—
To save!—'Tis well!

MOLAY (*who has heard* FRANK'S *speech with increasing emotion, and can no longer contain himself*).
                    My son,—son of my friend!
Thy father's but a croaker, and thou art
A true Brienne!—Praise God for that! But go
Dear lad, and lave thyself at yonder spring,
Then hie thee to the castle, there to take
Thy vow. Be sure thou art forthcoming,—go!
                              [*Exit* FRANK.
He has a heart,—is worthy of our league,
Thank God!

PHILIP.
Why, my dear Molay!—

MOLAY.
                    Shame, old doubter!—
There spoke his manly heart! And all his bells,
With all their jingling, deadened not the cry
Of suffering innocence—Whereof I am glad!

PHILIP.
I too. One jackal lives the less!—the youth
Has instinct!—

MOLAY.
          Let us not contend, but share
All delectation of this lovely hour.

PHILIP.
Will you not then to dinner?—It is time!

MOLAY.
Erewhile I was o'erfull of bitter feelings;
Now revel I in sweet ones,—Thank the Giver;
Oh Brother! could I dissipate, withal,
Thy clouds!—

PHILIP.
My sky was lost with Adalbert.

MOLAY.
" Dead also is Patroclus!"—Call to mind
The roundelay we in the forest sang
As boys so often. Thou Achilles wert,—
Patroclus I!—

PHILIP.
Oh, Youth!—Thou cruel friend,
Wherefore just now remind me of it, when
Renewed grief rages in my soul for *him*
With whom departed my last spark of youth!

MOLAY.
O be a man! See! Millions of fresh lives
Are slowly languishing 'neath tyranny's
Sirocco.—Weeping bitterly they call
On thee for succour, whilst thou selfishly
Dost naught but mourn thy dead!

PHILIP.
No less than they
I languish also.

MOLAY.
Help to rescue them.

PHILIP.
O Tyranny! with thine envenomed slaver,
Thine own, I would I could thy thousand heads
Poison, and in the blood of all thy slain—
My own son's blood—would I could see thee drown!
The tree's corona died with him, what can
The trunk do?

MOLAY.
Richly flowering shoots
For the new planting of our Eden can
It give us. Of our Order be thou Knight!—
Thou art a Peer of royal race, thou art

A Temple-brother, an Adept! Thy fate
The Ancient Brethren know : and many know
Thee personally, only never think
To find thee in this working garb. Disclose
Thyself unto the brethren—Philip's ban,
In Cyprus, cannot hurt a hair of thine.

PHILIP.
Ha, that I mock at!—Yet I cannot be,
And may not be, a Templar-Knight.

MOLAY.
       O, let
The ambrosial blossoms of our youth once more
Breathe round thee! When as yet we scarce were men,
Thou wert my brother. Be so once again
In holy sense! I journey forth—To whom
Leave I my new creation?—Can he act,
The veteran Grand-Commander? Let him bear
The name—but do thou carry on the work!—
And if it be God's will that I must fall,
To His most holy cause a sacrifice,
And for His Promised Land,—O then do thou
Complete what I began!

PHILIP.
     My friend, my brother!
The kernel of my life!—Thou only tie
That to this disenchanted earth still binds
My worn-out heart! For thy sake, once again
I might consent to plunge me in the whirl
Of this wave-tossed, upheaving, turbid vortex
Which falsely men call Life. But, vain the thought!
A solemn vow-debars me.

MOLAY.
     Ay! a vow?—
Astonishing!

PHILIP.
Yes, friend! without reserve

My fearful fate I will disclose to thee
Or else my heart must break indeed. That night
When Philip's hirelings barbarously dragged
Me—Prince of the blood, and his first favourite,
The only man in all his servile court
Who bore him loyal duty—dragged me forth
From my wife's side, who then had wrestled through
Twelve hours of labour-pains—My wife who died
Two days thereafter with a still-born son!—
(A dungeon held me when the ill news came;)—
When on a mere suspicion false and vain,
Untried, unsentenced, I was driven forth
To exile; when, to sum up all, I heard,—
In that same moment when at last the frost
Benumbed me, and by hunger overcome
I needs must beg for food, that my good son,
My only son, my Adalbert,—because
He loved a maid whom the licentious King
Had marked down for himself—by hired hands
Of murderers had fallen; then I swore
A dreadful oath to fling aside my birth,
With my upbringing, rank, nobility,
And nothing be but Man; nought would I be
But simply human, so to revel in
The full intoxication of revenge,
Until I cooled it in the tyrant's heart!

MOLAY.
Philip! Thou'rt horrible!

PHILIP.
　　　　　　'Tis but one blast
One feeble glimmer of the hellish fire
Within me! Grant me, friend, this blest relief,
One moment thus my heart, silenced so long,
So long repressed, to pour forth in a cry
Of rage to heaven!
　(*Falls sobbing on* MOLAY'S *breast; then after a pause, in
　　　which he has recovered himself*)
　　　　　　　　When through half Christendom,
Long time I'd wandered, and, repulsed by all,

Could find no roof, no cave, no tree, where death
With peace, might claim me, I engaged myself
As boatswain on a man-of-war. She went
Ashore by Cyprus—all the crew went down,
Three hundred vigorous young lives, and I
O, irony of fate! was saved. How then,
As Troubadour to Limasol I begged
My way and met thy friendly welcome,—how
Thou bad'st me call to mind our pact, and I
Forgot for one blest hour,—my happiest one—
All sorrows in my oldest friend's embrace!
O God!—Praise be to God!—Tears come at last.

MOLAY.

Let my kiss dry them!—Come into mine arms,—
Such moments are a sweet foretaste of Heaven.
[*Enter* GREGER.

GREGER.

The Grand Commander prays your Honour's presence.
Dinner is ready, and the Brethren all
Await you for the *Benedicite.*

MOLAY.

I will not eat.

GREGER.

    Which Ancient Knight shall say
Grace in your Honour's absence?

MOLAY.

        Ah, 'tis true!—
I'll come at once!   [*Exit* GREGER.
    'Tis thus I never live
One precious moment to myself alone—
Ah me! the Master's mantle!—It would press
Me down too sorely were it less sublime.
Philip, how much I envy thee thy spade!
When shall I too partake of blest repose,
And be, once more, plain mortal?—

PHILIP.
                        So let me
Remain then, and in garden-culture still,
(The work thou kindly gavest me thyself,
As balsam for my wounds,) forget that I
Was once myself a garden parasite!
Let me the picture of a quiet life,
With circumscribed horizon, still behold
Mirror'd in these sweet flowers, and, pondering o'er
Their forms renewed by Nature's boundless powers,
Forget how men demolish recklessly
The garden of their God within themselves.
Here too I somewhat aid thy purposes;
Thou mad'st me Garden-Brother, giving me
An office, in the Order, of high worth;
Lightly to loose the bandage from the eyes
Of every youthful neophyte that comes
To us, with gay chimeras all aglow,
And in this world of plants, where each as part,
Promotes, within its working-limits assigned,
The sure advancement of the garden's whole,
With all its might;—where high and low alike,
On pain of being uprooted, cheerfully
Partake the nurture of their fellow-plants;—
Your Temple's Holy of Holies show to them,
The nursing-cradle fair of human kind.
Let me proceed still further with this work,
Still love again in every vigorous youth,
Whose false self's stains I wash away for you,
The reflex of my dearly cherished dead!—
My brother, grant'st thou this?

        MOLAY (*seizing his hand with emotion*).
                Be gardener still!   [*Exit quickly.*

        PHILIP (*Alone*).
Thus ye young lives, I linger still with you!
Ah! could ye never more my peace renew?
Or must creative Nature always show
Destruction only to the sons of woe?   [*Exit pensive.*

SCENE III.

Prison: on the right a large iron door, on the left, more in the background, a smaller door.
The Ex-Prior of Montfaucon *(on one side of the front),* Noffo of Noffodëi *(on the other side, sitting at a table, upon which lies a guitar).*

PRIOR.
Noffodëi!

NOFFO.
Well, ex-Prior!

PRIOR.
No insults, knave!

NOFFO.
Ho! I'm as good a knight as you. We both
Are thrust together in one equal cell,
Save that you sit on that side, I on this.

PRIOR.
Thou wretched man! Must I ten times repeat
That 'twixt a villanous criminal and me,
Mere victim to an infamous cabal,
The distance is as great as earth from heaven?

NOFFO.
Ah, yes! You're here, because you'll not believe
A maid could be a mother; I, because
A fortress to the Sultan I betrayed
For twenty beggarly purses. 'Tis all one
And if betwixt us there be ought to choose,
Revenge steps in and makes us comrades sworn.

PRIOR *(starting up).*
Yes, yes, revenge, revenge! Forgive this once,

That I spoke scornfully!—'Tis true we pine
Together on one chain.—Sing me, good brother,
The song about the priest felled by the knight,
Which at nightfall the pilgrims sang to us
At Acre. I cannot recall it quite,
The end especially—

     Norro.
    Neither can I.

     Prior.
It sounds like fifes of Hell—the reason I
So long to hear it!—

     Norro.
   Always the same song!
Still, if it gives you pleasure I will sing it.
    [*Seizes the guitar, plays and sings, seated,
    during which the* Prior, *who stands
    before him, listens with every sign of
    inward rage.*

Knight Willibald rides at all speed from the fight,
 About the midnight;
The smart of his wounds is unceasing, and he
Puts spurs to his steed through the forest free.
 He speeds through the moon-ray bright,
 And thinks of his wounds all night,
Nought heeding the little stars' radiant light.

He came to the cross-road where midmost the wood
 A crucifix stood,
And there stood a nebulous priest by the way,
And "Greeting in God's name, Sir Knight!" did he say.
 "Stay, Sir Willibald," said, where he stood;
 "Thou'st o'er ridden thyself, 'tis not good!"
"Would'st thou stay me, pale spectre in hood?"

"And if I do stay thee, thy safeguard am I,"
 Was the priest's reply.
"Wounded thou wert 'neath the sun-ray bright,
Healing thou'lt find 'neath the cool moonlight,"
 Was the shimmering priest's reply.
 "Ride not so quickly by;
Thy aches and thy pains for a respite cry."

"I ask not repose, I'm not tired," said the knight,
  "But no more I'll fight.
Wounded sore, out of the battle I've come,
And I'll rest myself soon at my house at home,
  And no more in Crusades I'll fight."
    "But hast thou a dwelling-site?"
"'Tis Goldburg—" "Ah, there I had shelter one night."

"And how was my true wife? for news I am fain!"
    "She died in her pain."
"What sayest thou, priest?" "Thy children are dead.
Slain by thy foe in the evening," he said.
    "My sword shall pay back blood and pain
    When I come to my house again!"
"Thy house lies in ashes, an omen!—refrain!"

"Let me press on!" "But whither?" "To seek my foe!"
    "Thou'rt too weak to go,
Thy servants have all from thy retinue fled,
Thy friends are o'er all the land scattered and spread,
    Thou scarce for thy wounds can'st go."
    And e'en as the priest said so,
He broke the knight's lance at a blow.

"What doest thou, priest?" cried he desperately,
    And his sword grasped he;
The priest did but touch it, it snapped in two,
And all the knight's wounds began bleeding anew,
    But firm in his seat sits he,
    And spurs his horse savagely;
The horse falls dead; pale is the knight as can be.

Then out spake the priest—"To the Cross draw near:
    Thy shelter's here!"
"No Cross do I need—I suffice for myself,
Thou art nought but illusion, a warlock elf!
    This rock be my shelter here,
    This rock give me rest and cheer!"
The rock as he climbed fell in fragments, sheer.

So there lay the knight, and the priest to him ran;
    "Thou hapless man,
Disabled thou art, but one salve is sure,
Turn, turn thee to Jesus thy wounds to cure!"
    "Disabled, yet still a man,"
    Snarls the knight, and as best he can,
Strikes the priestling, who melts in a trice from his scan.

Thereat, ere his soul from his body went, jeered
    The knight in his beard:
"The priest's is the fault that my sword I lost,
But sweet is revenge, and his life it cost."

Every night with a bloody beard,
Still haunts he that rank; and feared
Is the Cross as he rides by it, raging and weird.

PRIOR.
" The priest's the fault." O, sing it once again,

PRIOR and NOFFO (*singing together*).
The priest's is the fault that my sword I lost,
But sweet—

EUDO (*passes unseen by the lattice and sings emphatically*).
Is the Cross to the tempest-tossed!—
He laughs in his beard every night,
But with tears!—And the Cross gives him light;
While the night-storm wings o'er him its flight.

[EUDO *goes on further. The sounds gradually cease.*

PRIOR.
What was it?

(*Enter* CHAPLAIN CYPRIANUS.)

NOFFO.
Ha! The greasy Cyprianus
Is making game of us!
[*Sportively rapping the* CHAPLAIN *on his bald head.*
Thou, rascal, thou!—

CHAPLAIN.
What ho! So jovial, sons of Belial?

PRIOR.
Ay!
So jovial are we that, wer't worth our while,
We'd strangle thee right off with our own hands.

CHAPLAIN.
Will nothing turn you from your evil ways?

PRIOR.
First turn thyself, thou cozener of men.

NOFFO.
What boots it quarrelling o'er the Emperor's beard ?[1]
Tell us some news, fat bald-pate, that we may
Have something fresh to vegetate upon
In our too quiet cell; for wanting that
One yawns one's life away, from sheer ennui.

CHAPLAIN.
News?—What?—You surely must have heard the story,
Known in the stable to the grooms already?

NOFFO.
Story?—What story?—

CHAPLAIN.
                    That the Holy Father,
Who now presideth o'er the Church's weal
At Poictiers, bids the Master join him there.

PRIOR.
We knew no syllable on't

CHAPLAIN.
              Is't possible?

NOFFO.
Ay, truly. In this thrice accursèd hole,
No note of Fame's hoarse trumpet penetrates.

PRIOR.
And what's the motive of this invitation?

CHAPLAIN.
To talk about a new Crusade, for which

---

[1] *German Proverb.*—Um des Kaisers Bart streiten, or spielen.
It was a disputed question whether Charlemagne ought to be represented with a beard or without. This proverb has its equivalent in all the languages of Europe.—*Trans.*

Our Master, and the Hospital's Master, who
Is also bidden, must to the Holy Father
Lend helping hands in word and deed.

     PRIOR.
         Ho! Ho!—
Is that the way of it?—The datery[1]
That fain would be regilding Peter's keys
Possesses nought but tinsel; so the tomb,
The holy tomb, must be ransacked anew.
A heritage 'tis they want, and no one can
Inherit from the living, therefore now
Must Christendom once more, with Cross on back,
Be hounded on the sabres of the Turks,
And feast on their good things. Upon my word
'Tis well devised; yet just a little played out!

     CHAPLAIN.
Oh, why yawns not the earth to swallow you,
Malignant, venomous heretic!

     NOFFO.
        What! not done
With wrangling?—*Dominus robiscum!*—Can't
You keep the peace, then, for a single hour?

     CHAPLAIN.
Peace, yes, forsooth! yon heretic merits not
That I should burn with zeal in his behalf!

     PRIOR.
Most miserable priest!

     NOFFO.
    Friend Chaplain, tell,
How came this news here?

     CHAPLAIN.
    By the packet-boat,

---

[1] The chancery of Rome, where the *datum Romæ* is affixed to the Pope's bulls.—*Trans.*

Which reached the haven early yester-morn.

PRIOR.
And what is Molay doing?

CHAPLAIN.
He convoked
This morn the Chapter. God have mercy on us!
What scenes there were! Not as beseems Christ's flock,
Like heathens they were shouting all together.

PRIOR.
What was determined?

CHAPLAIN.
Oh, the noise was such
A man could scarce distinguish his own voice;
The portly Marshal held his baton up
Full seven times, but none heeded. Norfolk was
Jet-black with spleen and venom. Wildung like
A German buffalo roared. Montreuil himself,
The constant-smiling, in his fury bit
A piece out of his mantle.

NOFFO.
What found they
To shout about?

CHAPLAIN.
Some shouted about England,
And others for the Order's rights; ay, some
Stooped, God be with us! even to urge that help
Should from the accursed Sultan be implored.

PRIOR.
And Molay?

CHAPLAIN.
Him you know. He always can

Control himself. He waited till the storm
Had spent its sharpest fury; then he rose
And slowly looked around him—calm and still!
But yet with eyebrows sternly knit. Right well
You know that look of his—It ever seems
To me as though he'd stolen it from the Saint
In Stephen's chapel.

PRIOR.
               Yes, I know that look
With which he captivates men's hearts.

CHAPLAIN.
                   Then he
Inclined his head and spoke. And yes, indeed,
He spoke most excellently—I myself
Could scarce have spoken better. Yes, he spoke
Of heroism, and that the time was come,
And we should now appeal to arms and fight,
Beloved brethren! So spoke he, and stretched
His hand out—and he said—

NORRO.
               Thou rainest words,
Fellow! my little complement of wits
Is, like the ark of Noah, almost drowned
In deluge of thy speech. Thy rainbow nose—
Oh, use it as a pledge to us that thou
Wilt leave off raining!

PRIOR.
           Well I comprehend
Of Molay's speech the meaning. He, proud man,
Desires to break the last link of the chain,
And, independent grown of all the world,
Insidiously attach the purple to
The linen mantle.

CHAPLAIN.
           He will not succeed.
(*Softly.*) Between ourselves!—Art sure no warder listens
Outside the door?

NOFFO.
              Fear nought.   E'en had he heard,
He'd be already asleep again ere now!

CHAPLAIN.
Look you! This good crusade, most necessary
It is to priceless Christendom, and our sins
Have much deserved that God's correcting rod
Should scourge us;—yet is this Crusade—how should
I put it into words?—Between ourselves—
But as the mantle is the pallium, 'sooth,
That overhangs the surplice.

          PRIOR (*with increasing attention*).
                    Plainer make
Your meaning.

CHAPLAIN.
          If you gentlemen will not
Betray me—

NOFFO.
   We? Such warm, devoted friends!

PRIOR (*Aside*).
Scoundrel!

CHAPLAIN.
          Then look you! the Provincial Father,
My reverend friend and patron, writes to me—
But secretly, as though under the seal
Of the confessional!—Hark ye, betray
My confidence, and ye shall one day roast
A longer spell by so much in Hell-fire!

          PRIOR (*Aside*).
Coarse, virulent numskull!

NOFFO.
                    We'll be silenter
Than e'en these prison walls.

CHAPLAIN.
                Then mark my words!
Thus Father Vincent writes: His Holiness
Is ill-affected to the Temple Order.
The Master, rumour runs, himself is not
Quite orthodox in dogmas of the Faith,
And has, in conflict with St. Bernard's rule,
Amassed great wealth wherewith to aggrandise
The Order, and e'en make it—God forfend!—
A standing menace to the Holy Father,
Perhaps, one day.

                PRIOR.
                Your noses are so fine,
It should be true. The dullest Priest scents out
The devil sooner than the sharpest layman
Can track him.
                CHAPLAIN.
                Therefore has the Holy Father
Only imagined a Crusade—You take me—
To inveigle hence the Master to Poictiers.

    PRIOR (*with an increasing, but restrained rage*).
I understand you, yes.

                CHAPLAIN.
                How easily
There, might aspiring Babel have a fall!

                PRIOR.
'Tis plausible! And did the cunning rogue
Write you aught else besides, in confidence?

                CHAPLAIN.
Why, yes! for this was Father Vincent's thought:
If something could be *proved* against the Order,
Of heresy, or violated oath—
You understand me?

                PRIOR.
                Yes, your quest is for

The primitive club, that only strikes behind,
And surely slays.

CHAPLAIN.
And so he thinks, if now
A pair of valiant and God-fearing men
Connected with the Order, could resolve
For their own good and for the Church's health,—

PRIOR.
Well!

CHAPLAIN.
And attest at Clement's judgment seat
All the abominable things the Order has
Already practised, equally with those
Which might be practised probably, 'twould have
Great weight—

PRIOR.
I can believe it!

CHAPLAIN.
(*Looking at them both askance, significantly.*)
Yes, indeed.
And certain men might find themselves set free
From charge of heresy, from dungeon air;
(*Looking at the* PRIOR.)
Some men might rise, should some events befall,
To posts of highest honour.

NOFFO.
Thou dost speak
Like Habakkuk. Come, here's a kiss for thee,
Thou archchaplain of all the cowled!
(*Throws his arms round him.*)

CHAPLAIN (*hastily*).
Then may
I to the Holy Father tell—

PRIOR (*bursting out in a rage*).
That I

Will send to Hell thy devilish embassy
And thee! What, Heribert! Hast thou then sunk
So low that this accurst, this shameless priest
Dare come to thee with messages like these?

CHAPLAIN.
Yet thou dost hate the Master?

PRIOR.
                                Abject worm!
Hate him I do, more bitterly than Hell,
But am not by my hatred made a villain.
These overtures are made me by the man
Whom James de Molay lifted from the mire,
And made for him the road to fortune free!
Ha! 'tis the first time that I do not grudge
The Master's mantle to thee, James de Molay,
Since snakes like these are warmed in it for thee!

CHAPLAIN.
Do but consider—
                PRIOR.
            Speak, accursed slave!
Wherefore would'st thou betray thy Lord and Master?
He's been as father to thee—that I know.
Wherefore betray'st thou him?

CHAPLAIN.
                        The Lord hath said,
"Thou shalt obey thy God rather than men!"
'Tis true that Molay has in temporal things
Dealt with me liberally, with sundry gifts,
But I am subject to the Church; if she
Demand his blood, I, faithful, with one hand
Bless him, and with the other immolate.

PRIOR (*who, without heeding the* CHAPLAIN'S *last speech, has
      been standing lost in thought, after a pause*).
Grave is the situation; yet I must,—
Revenge must yield to honour's high demands,
I must disclose this treachery to the Order.

CHAPLAIN (*Aside to* NOFFO).

Jesu Maria!

NOFFO (*Aloud to the* CHAPLAIN).
Let him have his way!
Could you prevent him? Wherefore should he not?
You've promised him, 'tis true, the dignity
Of Master, but he likes it not: he will
To Molay, his forgiveness to implore,
As guerdon for revealing all that you
Have trusted to his honour. And he'll succeed;
I'll wager Molay will at last entrust
Some little Priorate to him. And, friend Chaplain,
This course is much the wisest, for 'tis clear,
If Molay lives, will never Heribert
Be Master! That is clearly understood,
And plainly was evinced that time when he,
After Gaudini's death, so craftily
Snapped up the Mastership before his face![1]

PRIOR.

Ha! thank thee for reminding me of that!
Priest, I am silent, and I will forget
All that thy villany has revealed to me.
This I may justly do, since he from me,—
The worthier,—robbed the linen-mantle fair,
The prize so long desired, so long deserved;
And flung me, then—he, or his Chapter, 'tis
All one to me,—into this mouldering cell,
On the mere empty and exploded plea,
That I had called a sacred legend lies,[2]—

---

[1] The Grand-Master Gaudini, overwhelmed with sorrow and vexation at the loss of the Holy Land, and the miserable situation of his Order, stripped of all its possessions on the Asiatic continent, and destitute of houses to dwell in, died at Limesol after a short illness, and was succeeded by Brother James de Molay, of the family of the lords of Longvic and Raon, in Burgundy. Gaudini was appointed Grand-Master at Acre in 1291, after the death of William de Beaujeu from the arrows and darts of the enemy; and soon afterwards escaped, with a few Templars, to Cyprus. The remainder of the surviving 300 Templars were buried in the fall of the tower of the Temple at Acre, which was undermined by the Mamelukes.—*Trans.*

[2] "Answer me not," said the Templar, "by urging the difference of

While in his heart he mocks at it himself.
He derogates from duty: therefore I
Relax my duty also!
     CHAPLAIN.
    Praised be God!
Then you are with us?

     PRIOR.
   No. Whilst I draw breath,
I'll not degrade myself by such a compact.
Had James de Molay, sooth, slain wife of mine,
Murdered my first-born in the cradle, ay!
Or even called me liar, then fain would I
In open challenge kill him, and I could drink,
As a life-giving cordial, greedily
His heart's blood to replace the wine so long
Denied me; but with you to treat on terms
Of fellowship,—never shall Heribert
Achieve revenge at such a monstrous price.
You have my knightly word of honour on't,
I will keep silence; but conspire with you
I will not, never, never.—Let common clay
Ally itself with clay; the eagle still
Aspires to wing its way to loftier ends!   [*Exit*.

   CHAPLAIN (*after a pause, querulously*).
Well, Brother Noffo?

    Noffo (*imitating him*).
    Brother Cyprian?

our creeds; within our secret conclave, we hold these nursery tales in derision. Think not we long remained blind to the idiotical folly of our founders, who forswore every delight of life for the pleasure of dying martyrs by hunger, by thirst, and by pestilence, and by the swords of savages, while they vainly strove to defend a barren desert, valuable only in the eyes of superstition. Our Order soon adopted bolder and wider views, and found out a better indemnification for our sacrifices. Our immense possessions in every kingdom of Europe, our high military fame, which brings within our circle the flower of chivalry from every Christian clime—these are dedicated to ends of which our pious founders little dreamed, and which are equally concealed from such weak spirits as embrace our Order on the ancient principles, and whose superstition makes them our passive tools."—*Ivanhoe*, vol. ii., ch. ix.—*Trans*.

And have you driven your coach well up the hill?

CHAPLAIN.
I must confess—

NOFFO.
That, with the best of wills,
Your thick skull fails you in the accomplishment?
But fear you nothing.—Only set us free,
Forth of this place, and ship me off to France,
I'll answer for the Prior. His pride secures
Him to us. Thou can'st write?

CHAPLAIN (*Offended*).
I write!—I can
Engross, forsooth!

NOFFO.
Then write on thine own heart,
In characters engrossed, this short wise *dictum:*
"When as the Devil on easy terms can't get us,
He sends concupiscence and pride to fret us,
To the Devil, the Devil's power long since had flown,
Had he not set these scouts around his throne."

ACT III.

SCENE I.

The Hall of the Masters; the pillars and entablature are of blue marble; on the right the principal entrance, opposite it a niche, both framed in jasper; the niche is veiled by a blue [1] *curtain. Midway in the background stands the statue of the first Master of the Order, Hugo of Payens; on both sides of the hall, statues of the other five-and-twenty Masters, all life-sized in jasper—of which those which are more narrowly described in the scene following, are characterised by the attributes there ascribed to them.*

COMMANDER HUGO.   FRANK OF POITOU.

COMMANDER.

'TIS true, is't not, my dear young gallant? God mend it!
The Order's not so poor as it appears?

FRANK.

Amazed I view this splendid affluence,
Simplicity so wed with solid strength.—
Ennobled, hallow'd by the Cross of Christ,

---

[1] Blue is the colour of the Virgin Mary (*Stella Maris*, Star of the Sea), the name *Mary* implying the bitterness or saltness of the sea; and blue is expressive of the watery and moon-like principle, Isis.
The patroness of the Templars was "la doce mère de Dieu" (the sweet Mother of God). See "Secret Societies of the Middle Ages"; and in our Temple Church of London, which is dedicated to the Virgin Mary, the fundamental colour of the East window and of the adornments of the altar is blue.
This "Isis" principle was a great point with the Rosicrucians, with whose ideas there can be little doubt some of those of the Templars were closely allied.—*Trans.*

The strong heroic age appears to speak,—
A spirit blest,—in welcome kind to me,
From all these columns, all these cupolas.

COMMANDER.

Sheer truth thou sayest!—I am an aged man
And long I've dwelt within these castle walls;
No charm of novelty can influence me;
Yet oft, in these dim halls a shuddering takes
This breast unused to fear, and then meseems
As though the antique columns which have upborne,
Through ages, the dome's boldly curved concave,
Did call to me : " Be faithful unto death ! "
When I sometimes at evening-tide survey
The ancient tower in Gothic pomp ornate,
And see its ball that in the moonlight shines
Like some small star high in the firmament;
Then seems it me, the earlier knighthood, like
A giant-counterpart, peers down on me,
Immense and yet most comforting ; then is it
As though one whispered in mine ear : " 'Twas men
Piled up this bulk stupendous, by their zeal
And courage, and their living faith that they
Must give some holy gift, to overlive
The dust." Then I reflect how much men *might*
Achieve of good, and how, God mend it! they
So little *will;* amazed,—the pious race
Of valiant heroes could so dwindle down
To such a breed of earth-worms !—Then no draught
Of wine, no nice repast refreshes me;
I seem a stranger in this world of dwarfs:
I limp in sadness to my little room,
And groan to think I should have lived for this!

FRANK.

Methinks, excuse me!—you mistake the mist
Which heralds shining morn, for black midnight.
All yet may mend and take a better turn !—

COMMANDER.

It may ? God mend it! but it shall! it must!

We're sworn so much to Christendom!—But enough
Of this!—How pleaseth you this hall?

FRANK.

When one
Has left behind the Chapel's holy dusk,
And grand solemnity of choral chants,
And seen, in the refectory's bright array
Of garnished tables, well illustrated
The varied aspect of our daily life,
Then is it well in this grand hall to view
Such tender blendings of the grave and gay,
Together interfused with matchless skill.
The eye might fancy in these jasper forms,
That gleam so grandly from the marble's blue,
It saw the eternal Temple manifest,
And in the azure of high Heaven beheld,—
Irradiant in the Holiest's glorious light,—
All noble souls, to their best nature true,
Who to high Duty wholly gave themselves.

COMMANDER.

You read aright.—Around this hall they stand,
The illustrious Temple-Order's holy saints,
The Masters' sculptured forms from first to last,
Undaunted leaders in the work they loved.
In this same hall, when any Master dies,
His successor the elect thirteen must choose,[1]

   This is the old typical number, twelve, with its head, or thirteenth, which, beginning with the Sun and 12 Zodiacal signs, is repeated throughout the world's history: as in the 12 hours of the night assigned to Osiris as his companions and assessors, and personifying gods at whose head was Horus the rising Sun: as in the hero of the Babylonian epic, Iadubar, and his 12 great adventures: in Hercules the Sun-God and his 12 labours: in the Council of 12 of the Areopagus, under which were besides subordinate councils of 12; in the legend of Alexander and his 12 Cheders: in Odin and his council of twelve: in the 12 satyrs or wild men, appointed by the witch Kalyb to accompany St. George: in Arthur and his 12 Knights: in Charlemagne with his 12 peers, down to the electoral Chapter of the Temple with its Chief. This number was also chosen by the Sun of Righteousness to be that of his Apostles.
   However, in Act VI. Scene 2, which deals with the innermost ineffable mysteries of the Order, the number of persons engaged with them is brought down to the more deeply mystical number seven.—*Trans.*

Who, by their number, keep in memory that
Of Christ and his disciples; they must choose
Among our elders him who shall be named
Protector of the Temple, and those forms
Of eld look down in warning, and preside,
That no elector be by love or hate
Induced to give the preference to his friend,
Over some worthier brother, or to ignore
An enemy's deservings. They remind
Us all how absolutely needful 'tis
The Masters' mantle they with glory wore
Should never from a *fainéant's* shoulders hang,
Of duty and of honour negligent.
When thus the Master by established use
Is chos'n, the Electoral-Commander goes
Anew into his Chapter with his twelve,
And to the brethren says: "Beloved Knights, praise
Ye Jesu Christ our Lord, and our dear Lady,
Because that now, as ye have given command,
The Master we have chosen in God's name?
Are ye content with this that we have done?"
And all the brethren say with one accord,
"In God's name!" Thereupon the elect thirteen:
"Promise ye him obedience, all his life?"
Then all say—"Yes, with God's help, verily." Then
The Electoral-Commander speaks unto
The eldest Brother in such terms as these:
"Commander! if so be that God and we
Have chos'n thee out for Master, dost thou vow
True fealty to the Order all thy life,
And maintenance of good morals and good manners?"
Then answers he, "With God's help, yes!" The same
Questions the Electoral-Commander asks
Our ancient Brothers, second, third, and fourth;
And then to the elected Brother goes,
Calls him by name, and thus addresses him:
"I' the name of God the Father, Son and Spirit,
Brother, for Master we have chosen you.
You stand elected." To the Brethren then
Says, "Knights belov'd and Brothers, thank ye God!
Behold the Master!" These words said, at once

The Chaplain Brothers chant, with solemn choir,
Their loud *Te Deum*, the Brethren all vacate
Their stalls, and with great joy of heart take up
Their Master, whom they reverently bear
Forth to the Chapel, placing him in front
Of Christ's High Altar, that the Crucified
May look upon the man ordained of Him
To be the Order's head. Meanwhile intone
The pious Chaplains : " *Kyrie Eleison,
Christ' Eleison, Amen ! Salvum fac
Servum tuum,*" and so forth, which the Choir
Divinely echo back. Our Ancient Men
Then seize the Master, and enrobe him with
His mantle, then into this Master's Hall
Conduct. Then speaks the Eldest : " In God's name
Here show I thee the perfect counterfeit
Of men who have been better men than thou !
And if thou follow them, and, single-souled,
Display the Order's banner, thou shalt live ;
But if not so,—the Lord will thee forget,
And thy remembrance fade away from us."
Then says the Master : " As I have sworn to you
My vow I'll keep, so help me Jesus Christ !—
And these old men, the latchet of whose shoes
I am not worthy to unloose, shall all
Accuse me to my God, e'en as they now
Draw near the Lamb for me with saintly prayers,
If I deal other with you than I said."
Thereon the Marshal three times calls his name,
From every window to the assembled folk.
These things we use to do when we elect
A Master. And, thereafter, call this hall
Hall of the Masters.

     FRANK.
   'Tis a noble use !
Blest be that chosen one whom God promotes
To ornament this place !

    COMMANDER.
   E'en you too, might

Attain thereto, if diligently you
Would seek that holy thing the world knows not.
But I must point out to you, and explain,
The ancient statues—

      FRANK.
       Leave it, valiant Lord
And Father! You have already shown me all
The place! It is not well that you should stand
So long—defer it till another time!

      COMMANDER.
No! After dinner 'tis good to circulate.
Moreover, you're the son of old Poiton!
He was my comrade in so many a march
When not fatigue in question was, but death,
So faithful always at my side, that I
Can well afford to hobble with his son
A little longer than my usual wont.
See here (*pointing to* HUGO's *statue*) the ancient man with
  folded hands!
What do you think of him?

      FRANK.
       In these deep lines,
The steadfast eyes, the firm shut mouth, hair smooth,
As though anointed with God's peace, which ends
Long bearded, in the true Cross which his breast
So fences that it needs no other shield,
His lifting of the banner of the Cross,
Clasped in his folded and most virile hands,
And in his raiment's holy folds that hide,
In part, the armour beautified by it:
In the whole man, a Sage I see inspired
With holy strength to consummate the Right,
Himself a sacrifice without reward,
For Right's pure sake.

      COMMANDER.
      He is the founder of

Our Temple-Order, Hugo of Payens,'
First Master. Him the Spirit moved to leave
His fatherland, the lovely fields of France,
To suffer trouble, and want, and poverty,
But more to him than empty earthly joys
Was highest holiness. Thereto he sought;
He went, accompanied by eight more knights,
French-born, forth to Jerusalem in the year
Eleven hundred and eighteen, to found
The Order, those poor pilgrims to protect
Who journeyed to the Holy Land in faith.
Then swore they to the Patriarch Stephanus
The three vows of the rule canonical,
Poverty, chastity, and obedience.

   FRANK (*pointing to the pedestal of the bust*).
There stands upon the upper pedestal
A man's bust, crowned.

     COMMANDER.
      Our first protector, he
Baldwin by name, King of Jerusalem.[2]
He gave our Fathers, for a dwelling place,
His palace that stands eastward, close upon
Solomon's Temple: they were Temple-Knights,
And therefore Templars we still call ourselves.
This wise King also gave, well knowing how
From small commencements oft great things result,
Raiment unto our Fathers, food and drink,
And to their needs benignly ministered.
For Hugo boldly his great work began
Without house, clothes or food, with only trust
In God, he and his eight companions. Yes,
In those old times our Fathers were so poor

---

[1] Instituted in 1118. The Templars took monastic vows and engaged to defend the Temple of Jerusalem against the Moslems. Hugh de Payens, founder of the Order, recruited in Europe 300 knights of the noblest families. He was a native of Provence.—FROST, *Secret Societies*.

[2] Godfrey of Boulogne, in humility and reverence rejected the crown of gold, and was crowned with thorns in Jerusalem. Therefore Baldwin, his brother, who succeeded him in two years, entitled himself, *Rex Hierusalem, Latinorum primus.*—*Trans.*

That two must ride together on one horse,[1]
And so 'tis graven on the Order's seal—

    FRANK (*still lingering by the pedestal*).
And now, this other bust? 'Twould seem a monk,
Although his open mouth, his fiery eyes
Seem half from the old Roman Cicero,
And half from Kaiser Karl the Great derived.

      COMMANDER.
That is the pious and most eloquent
Abbot of Clairvaux.[2]
      FRANK.
    Ha! is that indeed
The holy Bernard!
      COMMANDER.
    None but he. At Troyes,
At the Church Council, he himself drew out
The Order's holy Rule; on Hugo's breast
He hung the Order's habit, the mantle white
With the red Cross. Much he rejoiced that we,
Few as we were, were willed to consecrate
Our life-blood to defend the holy tomb
Whose rescue was his only dream, himself
Forgot. To those Princes and Lords impelled,
By God's voice in him, forth to the Crusade,
He us commended, and the Patriarch's soul
Impressed that he should open all his heart
To these preservers of the Church.
  (*Pointing to the two others next in order on the pedestal
    of the statues.*)

---

[1] The emblem of a winged horse, which is seen all over the Temple-Church, is thought to be the time-corrupted image of the two Templars on one horse. This, at least, is one interpretation. But, knowing how largely the Crusaders flooded Europe with myths of the Orient, we may, with equal fairness, see in it the "Winged Horse of Kurdistan" (recognized by the Greeks as Pegasus), of which St. George's horse of miraculous velocity was, no doubt, the antitype.—*Trans.*

[2] Clairvaulx is situate among the woods near Bar-sur-Aube in Champagne. Bernard its Abbot became in many ways the oracle of Europe; he chiefly shone in the proclamation of the second Crusade. His preaching was a triumph of eloquence and zeal.—*Trans.*

                         The third
And fourth are sovereigns both; that represents
Henry the first of England, this, the first
Alphonso of Navarre. The Founder this[1]
In London of the Templar-House; and that
Bequeathed his kingdom to us; but his heirs
Annulled his promise, in accord with God's
Wise providence, think I : for God the All-wise
Appoints us not for rulers of mankind,
But as mankind's exemplars, that we may
Be to all people as a shining light,
Shining in darkness.

   FRANK (*pointing to another statue*).
      Who's the stalwart man
With high plumed helmet, from whose countenance
Gleams forth a hero's spirit?

   COMMANDER.
      He is Bernard
Of Tremelai, fifth Master; a brave man,[2]
But too fool-hardy quite to have deserved
The name of hero. For, true courage is
But vassal unto wisdom : valour is
The fief it holds of her; but should it too
Audaciously transgress its vassalage,
Itself and others it to ruin hurls.
So Tremelai when, with his Templars, he
Camped before Ascalon; there skilfully
A lofty wooden tower on wheels he built
And in the Saracens' teeth, who vainly strove
To ignite it, Bernard made a breach, and through
The opening gallantly with forty Knights
Made his resistless way into the town.
But all too keenly he pursued his foe,
And space for conflict failed him in the fight;
And, so befell it, the whole forty fell
With him to his rash deed a sacrifice.

---

[1] Haydn, "Dict. of Dates", says the Templars came to England early in Stephen's reign, and settled at the Temple in London; and at other places in the reign of Henry II.—*Trans.*

[2] A Burgundian.—*Trans.*

FRANK (*going up to another statue*).
And now this other, with the cockle-hat,
And pilgrim staff?—

COMMANDER.
           The seventh he; Andrew
Of Montbarri, to great Saint Bernard kin,
Who loved him dearly and foretold to him
His dignity as Templar. Thus he wrote:
"You say, perhaps, with Jacob—nought had I
Beside this staff when I o'er Jordan passed,
And now I lead three bands."—It came to pass
As said. He who a needy pilgrim came
To join the Order, was our Temple's Master,
And nought ashamed to own his former life
Of indigence, chose thus to be portrayed.
For then 'twas to a Christian's praise to rise
By self-exertion from his lowliness.
Now, if some David, of a thousand, lift
Himself above the Throne, or under it,
He gilds with tinsel-gold his shepherd-pouch,
That in the rank may be forgot the man.

FRANK.
So was the nephew of the uncle worthy!

COMMANDER.
Thus, by his uncle's fatherly advice,
Became he Templar, and no prince's thrall.
"Woe to our Princes!" Bernard wrote to him,
They bring to pass no good thing in God's land,
But follow rapine and iniquity.
What power they have they put to evil use;
The good they might do, understand they not.[1]

FRANK.
I hope with some exceptions.

COMMANDER.
           Yes, God mend it!

---

[1] To those who know the history of the Order, it is superfluous to remark, that all these traits, together with the above description of the Masters' Election, are in accordance with historical facts.

FRANK (*turning to another statue*).
Who is that spare, emaciated man,
The ninth there, in the Masters' circle? He
Looks down with gaze so earnest, so sublime,
As though he would not buy the world itself
At cost of the most trivial peccadillo!—
Why weareth he a chain on his left foot?

COMMANDER.
Bow down before him! The great Odo 'tis
De Saint Amand, Martyr to righteousness.
After a long life fruitful in great deeds,
At Belfort, where he like a lion fought,
He fell a prisoner to Saladin.
The Sultan's wish was to exchange him for
His favourite cousin, by the Christians ta'en,
In that same action. Odo then proclaimed:
"There is an ancient statute of our Order,
By force of which no ransom may be given
For any captive of our fellowship
Save knife or girdle. And upon this law
Rest the foundations of the Order, for
Each one thus dies a hero's glorious death,
Since such a price avails not to redeem.
This law relaxed, its influence soon declines.
Saladin will not for such ransom loose
My bonds: So be it! in prison I will die!"
He said, and steadfast as a rock remained.
Weeping the Elders from the dungeon went,
And Odo died starvation's lingering death.

FRANK.
Oh, how I pity him!—

COMMANDER.
                    Not such should be thy cry,
First live for Righteousness, and then for Duty die!
Your senses mortify, to vivify your spirit;
The Temple's guardianship the Templar-Knights inherit!—

ROBERT (*rushing in impetuously, without noticing* FRANK).

H

ROBERT (*addressing himself throughout to the* GRAND-COMMANDER).
Commander! joy!—I've taken the Tunisian!

COMMANDER.
Where wert thou at the Chapter-hour to-day?

ROBERT.
Hear you not, then?—I bring you the Tunisian!

COMMANDER.
Where wert thou at the Chapter-hour to-day?

ROBERT.
I was—out in the forest, watching for
The tiger, but a better prize I bring!

COMMANDER.
Though duty called thee to the Chapter-watch!

ROBERT.
I heard upon my way the turn was mine,
But thought—(*as the* GRAND-COMMANDER *is going to interrupt him impatiently*)
Permit me speech. A substitute
Can do this trifling service—often does,—
And leaves me rougher work. So it befell!—
The news came that the Turks had anchored. I
Could not endure this; forth I rushed in haste,
And six young giants followed where I led.
We couched ourselves in ambush on the beach,
And soon saw Turks who with their Captain came
Ashore, the fortress to investigate.

COMMANDER (*hastily interrupting*).
How many?—

ROBERT.
Well, I did not number them.

COMMANDER (*irritably*).
God mend it!—

ROBERT.
　　　　They were quite enough for us,
And we for them!—We charged them, in God's name,
And cut down with our sabres all we could.
By my spear wounded in his shoulder-blade,
The Captain yields. The others follow suit.
We towards the bastion go; the Turkish flag
Displays its crescent in full sight of the fort;
The ship's crew rush towards us with drawn swords;
"Surrender!" loud I cry, and lay my sword
Upon the Captain's breast. They yield themselves.
The Under-Marshal looked on while we fought.
When all went well, he came. Into his charge
The prisoners we confided, with their ship,
Only the Officer I bring you, and four
Enfranchised Christians. Will you see them now?—

COMMANDER.
Robert! thy deed, e'en though thy gallantry
Doth credit to the Order, is threefold
Subject to penance, by the Order's rules.
Thou didst forsake the Chapter-watch to-day
At thine own pleasure, that is punishable;
Thou hast hunted with thy hounds wild beasts, although
It stands commanded that a Templar Knight
Should only hunt the Devil out from his heart,
Not the poor wildings in the forest-chase..
That's punishable also. Finally,
Thou hast, without permission given by me,
The Master, and the Chapter, faced the foe.
Hast brought seven Templars, (a most serious thing)
Well-nigh to put to shame, by bootless deaths,
The Cross's banner, through thy recklessness;
So art thou trebly punishable.—Thou
Deserv'st to lose a year and day, thy mantle.

ROBERT (angry).
And call you those the statutes of our Order?—
If gallant courage—I must boast myself
Thereof, howe'er unwillingly—be crime,
Then, thou deceitful mantle, fare thee well!
　　　　　　　　　　[*Tears off his mantle.*

Thou once adorn'dst heroic brotherhood,
Now art thou nothing but a monkish cowl;
And that I care not for—so take you it!
  [*Throws the mantle at the feet of the*
    COMMANDER.

COMMANDER.
Robert, take up thy mantle!—Think, reflect,
What thou art saying! Be of better mind!

ROBERT.
I will not have it, and what I've ceased to will—
The Devil himself compels me not to will.

COMMANDER (*getting excited*).
Ho! Dost thou reverence the Commander thus?
Thou—rascal, thou?

ROBERT.
          A rascal!—Yet, because
Of your grey hair, and for your office' sake,
I'll take it from you.

COMMANDER.
          Yes, again a rascal!
Three times a rascal! craven dastard, too!
For he who has not courage to restrain
His idle thirst for fame beneath the yoke
Of duty's just a dastard, so God mend it!—

ROBERT (*breaking out in fury*).
I, dastard, I? Thou insolent grey-beard,
Thou hast not said all that to me for nought!
  [*He seizes the* COMMANDER *on the breast,
    and tears the belt from his mantle.*

FRANK (*who springs forward and tries to keep him off*).
Bethink you, Knight, unhand him! Let him go!

COMMANDER.
Together { You drag the sacred belt from off my mantle!

ROBERT.
He who assails my honour, murders me!

MOLAY, *accompanied by several* KNIGHTS, *comes up*.

MOLAY.
What loud outcry!—Why, Robert? what is this?

ROBERT.
Pardon me, Master!—But the Grand-Commander
Assailed me with the most insulting words;
My indignation then o'ermastered me!

MOLAY.
Commander?

COMMANDER.
In the Chapter will I speak!
(*After a pause.*)
He failed to fill his post at Chapter-watch;
He went forth hunting in the forest wilds;[1]
Without superior orders, he has seized
The privateer;—when I an aged man,
In right of my high office, censured him,
Straightway his mantle he insultingly
Threw down before me, seized me on the breast,
And tore from me the Order's holy belt.—
Now speak his sentence!

MOLAY (*with suppressed emotion*).
Robert! Punishment
Thou hast incurred. Not only forfeited

[1] It was one of the fundamental rules of the Institution, that no Knight should go hunting or fowling. "They are forbidden to take one bird by means of another, to shoot beasts with bow or arblast, to halloo to a hunting-horn, or to spur the horse after game. But, now, at hunting and hawking, and each idle sport of wood and river, who so prompt as they in all these fond vanities?"—*Amador*, vol. iii., ch. 5.—*Trans.*

Hast thou thy mantle; thou'rt in interdict,
And meritest, at least, to be expelled
The Order. Give to me thy sword!

     ROBERT (*gently*).
          Since you
Demand it (*more hotly, glancing at the* COMMANDER *and* FRANK),
    Else the Devil himself should not
Have wrenched it from me.

     MOLAY (*sharply and sternly*).
        Thou hast lost thyself!
    (*To two* KNIGHTS.)
Take him away!—
     [ROBERT *goes away quietly with the two*
     KNIGHTS.

    COMMANDER (*recovering from his choler*).
     A curious fellow that!

     MOLAY.
You are avenged—although I fain had wished
You'd been more tolerant of the youthful hero!
     (*To a* KNIGHT.)
Where is the privateer?

     KNIGHT.
      He waits without.
There is, among the rescued Christian slaves,
A gentleman, a Knight of France, 'tis said.

     MOLAY (*to the* KNIGHT).
Admit the prisoners to the audience-hall.
 (*Softly to the* GRAND-COMMANDER, *pointing to* FRANK).
Hast thou made ready the Recipiend yet?

     COMMANDER.
I have prepar'd him.

     MOLAY (*to* FRANK).
      Go thou to thy cell;
Prepare thee for the holy midnight watch. [FRANK *goes.*

[*A TUNISIAN PRIVATEER (with bandaged shoulder) is brought in by a KNIGHT; behind, a TROUBADOUR with a harp, ADALBERT OF ASOC, and two other PRISONERS of the Tunisians*).

MOLAY (*in the TUNISIAN*).

What are you?

TUNISIAN.
I? A gallant officer
Of Turks, confessing most unwillingly
Unto a Christian dog.

MOLAY.
The abusive term
But does me honour—Who are these with you?

TUNISIAN.
A couple o' hounds of no account, unless
To be spiked up upon the walls of Tunis.

MOLAY.
How came they in thy hands?

TUNISIAN.
At Cadiz, I
Had come across a Spanish frigate, laden
With a whole cargo of such knaves as these.
The Captain yielded like a caitiff slave,
Albeit his force was thrice the strength of mine,
So took I them; but soon that ballast proved
Too heavy a load, therefore at Tripolis
I trafficked all the worthless trash away,
Reserving these four to amuse myself
And win diversion from their foolish ways.
Thus towards Aleppo I had turned my course,
Intending them as gifts for the Pasha!
But then I thought I'd also take with me
A few white hides of these your Templar dogs.
I climbed to land; but there my evil star
Launched on me quite the best of thy sleuth-hounds;

The fellow had a sword, by Mahomet!
The Dey of Tunis strikes not better blows!—
The rest thou know'st. Dismiss me now and thrust
Me into narrowest cell, if only there
I may scent out no savour of the Cross.
Foul is its wood and shines but in the dark. (*Shuddering.*)
Ugh!—At its very mention I am seized
As with an ague—

MOLAY.
Silence, thou blasphemer!
And who art thou, old man?

TROUBADOUR.
A minstrel, Sir,
Who many a lay to Knights and lordly Counts
Have sung in Burgundy and Flanders, till
Old age approaching, my poetic gift
Began, alas! to dwindle; then to Spain
I wandered, to the home of noble song,
To warm myself amidst her wreathing vines,
To sun myself beneath her lucid sky.
There smiled on me once more the tuneful Muse,
But folly moved me, and I chose myself
A little youthful wife in nuptial bonds,
Beauteous as day, but shrewish as the fiend.

TUNISIAN.
The old tune—

MOLAY.
Interrupt him not.

TROUBADOUR.
Alas!
Dear Master, what a bitter change! Before,
I had through fifty swiftly fleeting years
Rejoiced me in the golden gift of song,
Glad as a child on holy Christmas eve;
Before, I seemed to reign o'er earth and heaven;
When I in forest chase, on vine-clad slope,
Did hail the rosy dawn, the twinkling star,—

In kindly unison, vine, streams, and tree
Seemed all to call to me, "Exult with us!"
Then I, a humble citizen, appeared,
In mine own eyes, a world-creative God;
And such in moments of my ecstasy
In truth I am! but that, when it is past,
Is like a dream and I myself know not
What then I dreamed; back into nothingness
I sink again and am as fibreless,
As simple as before.

TUXIBIAN.
Fool's paradise!

TROUBADOUR.
Most exquisite!—Ere yet the day with cheeks
Sleep-reddened, peered forth on the world, and woke
Lightly, with rosy finger-tips, the Sun,
His dear birth-giver, forth I roam'd with hair
Loose flowing, and bared neck, through villages,
Through towns, o'er hills and dales. In palace now,
And now in Sæter-hut, by great and small
Welcomed with hearty kindness, I to-day
Passed through the fields of Provence that I might
To-morrow in the glaciers mirror me,
Then on the next day, from the Vatican,
With awe survey the tomb of earthly greatness.
My mother-art seemed to support me e'en
As doth a hen her chicks. No care was mine
To seek me out a lodging, which each friend
Art-loving, and all trees, provided me.

MOLAY.
Never at home then?

TROUBADOUR.
                    Ah! an artist's life
Is but a pilgrimage. No spot on earth
Is his abiding place—a priceless gem
Still draws him on, which visible to sense,
Yet unattainable, before him floats.—

Alas! that I forgot it!—Foolishly,
I longed for home and hearth, for sweet repose,
And won it, but 'twas like a churchyard's rest.
My Hippogriff, by Hymen's bridle curbed,
Soon drooped his ears like a prosaic ass.
I, wretched man, the lyre laid by, must now
The distaff take, must hew me my own wood.
With worry and plague, instead of blissful joy,
At evening must I cower behind the hearth,
And, for the nightingale's sweet choral song,
Must hearken to the chatter of old wives.
But, by good fortune came a Knight our way,
And stole my spouse and all my worldly pelf,
And I was from my fetters free once more;
For property and women are the chains
Which drag us down from Helicon to dwell
'Mid earthly fustian.—I to Cadiz strolled,
And so took ship, with maravedis few,
But with a heart divinely rich, to sail
For Palestine, and carol there my hymn
To the Redeemer.

MOLAY.
           Try, meanwhile, our house;
Here too, you will find the heavens—and a heart.

TROUBADOUR.
I thank thee; and, if heard my wish, with favour
The gods shall smile on thee, nor ever waver;
Earth-discords, changed to silvery strains, depart
From him who loves the minstrel and his art.
                              [*Exit cheerfully.*

MOLAY (*to the* OTHER PRISONER).
And who art thou?

SECOND PRISONER.
           A cobbler I from Windsor.
I could not bear that Parliament abridged
The privileges of my craft.   So I
A hole punched in an Aldermanic head;

For this they'd fain have hung me, so I fled
To Calais in a little bark, and thence
Tramped on until at Cadiz I arrived,
And put to sea in that same hapless frigate
Seized by this (*pointing to the* TUNISIAN) Jew-like trafficker
    in men.

                  TUNISIAN.
Cobble he would the shoe political,
The corporate State-cobblers then seized him.—
There's nought but cobbling 'mongst you Christian dogs;
And what all cobble at, you call a State.

              MOLAY (*to the* THIRD PRISONER).
And thou?

                THIRD PRISONER.
        I am a man experienced much
In tapestry and divers rarities.
'Twas said that in the Egyptian pyramids
(This earnestly I beg you'll not reveal!)
A piece of Jacob's famous ladder, might
Be seen worked up in some material rare;
And thither I was going (for no expense
I grudge that takes me to the beautiful!)—
I wished also to measure by mine own ears
Whether the ancient Sphinx (as privately
Was told me, and I beg you'll keep it dark)
Has veritably ears so long that they
Are longer still than mine. And finally,
The mummies of old Pharaohs I would see,
Which still must much of their old savour reek.
(That smell, much as I've smelt, I much desire.)
With my own nose I longed to sniff them out,
The ancient Pharaohs—

     TUNISIAN (*hitting the* PRISONER *on the nose*).
                      Fool!—Sniff at thyself!
For thou art deader than those mummies are!

MOLAY (*pointing to* ADALBERT, *who stands in the background dejected and hanging his head; to the* TUNISIAN).
And what young man is this whose wasted cheek
Bears signs of much deep-seated inward grief?

     TUNISIAN.
An excellent youth! i' faith a pity 'tis
He may not come into the Pasha's harem
To be the women's darling! All the day
He spends in sighing. Does the moon light up
A little, in the twinkling of an eye
He flies to his guitar and sings a lay
Of his lost sainted Agnes, oh! so sad,
That even my rough heart's been stirred by it.
   (*To* ADALBERT, *taking him by the chin.*)
Come, Adalbert, cheer up! for here in truth
Thou art amongst thy co-believers.

    MOLAY (*to* ADALBERT).
          Come
Nearer to me, young man! (*Aside.*)
        A haughty mien!
How noble!—with a sweet sad dreaminess!—
I feel as if already I had seen
These features somewhere! (*Again to* ADALBERT.)
       Thou'rt named Adalbert?

     ADALBERT.
At dawning of my sultry earthly day,
They called me Adalbert of Anjou—

    MOLAY (*astonished*).
        Anjou?
  [*The* COMMANDER (*who, without attending
   to the preceding conversation, has been
   standing all the while immersed in
   thought, looking sometimes at* HUGO's
   *statue, sometimes at the niche, now
   becomes attentive*).
Son of the Constable?

MOLAY (*with eager inquiry*).
          The banished Duke?

ADALBERT (*sighing deeply*).
Ah! yes! You see in me the hapless heir
Of the unfortunate Duke of Anjou!

MOLAY (*losing all his self-control*).
                    Ha!—
Praise be to God! (*collecting himself, aloud to the* COM-
     MANDER).
          My honoured Eldest Brother,
Conduct the prisoners to the dining-hall;
I will detain this youth.

COMMANDER (*to the others*).
(*Goes with* TUZEMAN, BOTH PRISONERS, *and the* KNIGHT.
          Come! Follow me!

MOLAY.
(*Taking* ADALBERT *kindly by the head, and kissing him.*)
Oh dear young friend, most welcome! come at once
Into the garden!   [*Hurries him out.*

ADALBERT (*astonished*).
     Why?

MOLAY.
          Ask not, but come!—
Oh, blessed day! when I with interest can
Repay my friend's devotion!—Come, at once!
          [*He drags out with impetuosity the still
               astonished* ADALBERT.

SCENE II.

(The further end of the Temple Garden: on the left in the foreground the gardener's cottage, and in the background a mountain; between both, a view of the sea. The scene is illuminated by the last rays of the evening sun, soon about to fade into the darkness of night.)

    PHILIP *(alone, standing before his cottage).*
How glorious sinks the sun into the sea—
A flaming ruby on the purple rim
Of quickly fading day. The exulting waves
In all his undiminished beauty's might
Engulf him. So in fulness of his strength
My own sun set—He set at highest noon.
Alas! my Adalbert!
      [*Lies down on a plot of turf in front of the cottage.*
    Here will I sleep
This lovely night. Oh, would that when I wake,
This shell thrown by, in yon pure ether's blue
I might enfold him to my tortured heart!
          [*Goes to sleep.*

The TROUBADOUR *(comes in from left to right, strolling towards the hill; plays on the harp and sings to it).*

 Why hastens the sun, his cheeks all aglow with their jubilant fire,
  Down—down to the wave?—
 See!—in the deep to still, deliquated, his anxious desire,
  He leaps to his billowy grave!—
 Then with the exquisite anguish he's filled of complete separation,
  For ever to part;
 The sea closes over beneath, and, rich beyond all estimation,
  He falls on his Father's heart!—

    [*Goes away, the harp-tones gradually lost in the distance.*

MOLAY and ADALBERT (*appear in the background in front of the hill*).

MOLAY (*who comes on the scene leading* ADALBERT *by the arm,—eagerly, Aside*).
Where hides the old man?

ADALBERT.
                    Venerated Sir,
Forgive my asking—whither must I go?

MOLAY.
Nay, go yet further forwards; soon thou'lt see—
            (*Aside, perceiving* PHILIP.)
Ha! there the old man sleeps. I must prepare him;
A sudden joy might kill him—Hark! dear youth!
            (*To* ADALBERT, *still speaking quickly.*)
Go thou a little on that side, among
The shrubs—I'll call thee soon!—

ADALBERT (*perceiving* PHILIP).
                    There lies a man
Asleep, 'neath yonder tree!—

MOLAY (*pushing him on with good-humoured eagerness*).
                    Well, let him sleep!—
But go, my youngster, go!

ADALBERT (*immovable, looking at* PHILIP).
                    A fine old man
He seems to be, by his long silver hair!

MOLAY (*still eagerly trying to get him away*).
Yes truly! yes;—but go!

ADALBERT (*gently resisting* MOLAY).
                    I know not why,—
Like one that's rooted to the soil, I stand,
A thrill of expectation shakes the frame
Of my whole being—such terror and such bliss
Vibrate in me, I almost long to clasp
The evening-glow and press it to my heart!

MOLAY.
Away! Thou wilt feel better amid the shrubs.

ADALBERT (*still looking longingly at* PHILIP, *whilst he tries to free himself from* MOLAY).
I cannot, cannot part from that old man,
He draws me as with superhuman might—
Good Master! let, oh, let me see his face!

        MOLAY (*with emotion, letting him go*).
Go, enter then thy Heaven!—

ADALBERT (*having hastened from the background, where both had been standing, to the sleeping* PHILIP *in the foreground, and recognized him*).
                      Jesu! Maria!—
My father!

        PHILIP (*awaking, and still half asleep*).
        Help!

           ADALBERT.
            Yes, help I bring indeed!—
Oh, it is he,—'tis he!

           PHILIP.
        Ha!—

       ADALBERT (*warmly embracing him*).
                It is I!
Thy son's heart beats on thy dear heart once more!
Alas! he faints!

    PHILIP (*who had hitherto stared strangely at* ADALBERT, *feebly raising himself*).
        My Adalbert!

          ADALBERT.
                My father!

MOLAY (*who has been standing on the other side of the foreground, lost in joy as he surveys the group, with eyes raised to Heaven*).
My God, Thou hast been merciful to us!

The TROUBADOUR (*comes back from his ramble over the mountains in the background, singing as he goes, without remarking the persons present, accompanying himself with his harp*).

   With winglets twain drooped over,
   The Father doth us cover,
   Gladness and guilelessness;
   And when night's shades been dreary,
   He visits the life-weary,
   With comfort, peace, and Heaven's repose to bless.

    [*He goes—the harp-tones resounding back.*

ACT IV.

(The following day, towards evening.)

SCENE I.

(Prison—At one side a table.)

ROBERT *(without sword, hat, or mantle, sits dejectedly at one side of the table).* GOTTFRIED *(keeping guard over him, sits on the other side of it).*

GOTTFRIED.
HOW could'st thou then so far forget thyself?
 Our pride, the Master's friend and favourite?

ROBERT.
'Tis done!

GOTTFRIED.
 Why need'st thou be so goaded by
A word from the old irascible Commander?

ROBERT.
Ask me no further—Human nature's but
A cobweb,—vehement passion's not man's work,
It is his Genius' breath that circulates,
Unseen, its threads among, the faithful slave
Of Fate eternal; from the common dust
He cleanses them, dust that would earthward press
The web-work down—Let Fate but nod, at once
The little breeze to whirlwind grows, and rends

To shreds the web we fondly dreamt we'd spun
To last for ever-more.

          GOTTFRIED.
              Yet none the less
Man is the moulder of his destiny!

          ROBERT.
Impotent being! Can'st comprehend the words
Thy lips repeat?—Has that old myth of Force
And free Volition, which at the atom mocks,
And at annihilation, and which drives
By laws methodical the car of fate,
Re-echoed o'er to thee? Dream'st thou indeed,
Thou molecule! that thou and men like thee,
And tenfold better men than thou or I,
Could by a hair-breadth's space avail to turn
The wheel of fate from its eternal track?
I too have had such dreams; but terrible
Has been my wakening! See our Order!—lo!
How many thousands has it sacrificed
To further its high aim—And is it won,
That Promised Land?—Behold our Master's hair
Grown grey! the fruit of vigils of the night,
Of days spent fighting, of an ardent heart
Broken, though never cooled from its desire.
Sixty long years that noble heart has beat
In vain, and his creation's but a fair
Illusion, dreamt of by his lovely soul;
It dies with him! In vain will pilgrim seek,
Years hence, the spot where sleeps the noble dust.

         GOTTFRIED (*yawning*).
Yet has the Christian meed of heavenly joy;
And in his flesh he shall behold the Lord.

          ROBERT.
In flesh!—Good luck upon the journey then!
Thou'st but to stow it on the Angel's back
Who to eternal glory bears thee off.—
And may thy most delightful memories
Of precious hours when, at refection time,
Thou hast enjoyed good cheer, or groomed thy mare,

Or scoured thy rusted armour, and so forth,
Go with thee there and not be left behind!
Ah, self-deceiving race of man! Is't not
Enough for you that, at each step you take,
This carcase should oppress and hem you in,
That tooth-ache, head-ache, gout, what not besides,
At every turn degrade the lord of earth
To equal rank with cattle?—Will you take
This medley, of all elements the rude
Abortion, which lays bare, beneath the ray
Of light that strikes upon it from on high,
Its nakedness the more disgustfully :—
With all its freakish eccentricities,
That blister-like are bubbling in your blood,
And which you by such splendid names baptize,
Into your heaven?—By all means, take it then!—
    (*As his glance casually falls on* GOTTFRIED, *who has
        meanwhile fallen asleep.*)
Asleep already?—Well! To pigmy folks
All's lullaby—Ay, e'en these rattling chains!

ASTRALIS (*entirely covered by a red mantle which hides her
face, has glided in during the last sentence, and unre-
marked by* ROBERT *where he sits, has placed herself close
behind him; now taking him by the shoulders with both
hands*).
A man and—chains?

        ROBERT (*starting from his seat*).
        Who's there?
    (*Clasping the figure when he perceives it.*)
        A spirit embodied!
    [*He tears away the mantle and recognizes*
      ASTRALIS *standing before him in her
      usual cloister-dress.*

    ASTRALIS (*very earnest and with sublimity, now, and
        throughout the scene*).
                            Knight!

  ROBERT (*taking off his hands from her, and sinking back
      sorrowfully in his chains*).
    Thou com'st?

ASTRALIS.
I must go hence and would take leave to-night!

ROBERT.
Ah, whither?

ASTRALIS.
Through the land of tears to the Valley of peace intense.

ROBERT.
I,--prisoner ever!--

ASTRALIS.
    Strife for thee, then rest and quiescence!
After victory only, the Palm sweets exhaleth,
O'er bough and o'er blossom the tempest prevaileth;
But the tower that trouble builds never will cease
To mock at the storm,—in the Valley,—the sun-lighted
    Valley of peace!—

ROBERT.
Can I trust thee?

ASTRALIS.
As those that send me surely.—

ROBERT.
My spirit soars!

ASTRALIS (*Aside, with fervour*).
    To Mother Isis' throne!

ROBERT (*with returning, but softened sorrow*).
We part?—

ASTRALIS (*to him in her original tone*).
    Held by our Mother's hands securely.

ROBERT.
And what for me?

ASTRALIS.
    The Valley and (*Aside, with infinite tenderness*).
    Astralon!

ROBERT.
The Valley?—

ASTRALIS (*again earnest and solemn*).
Ask not, deeds dispense thou purely,
Give, not for meed or fame, thyself alone!—
First wonders work, would'st them unveiled be seeing,
And so achieve the fulness of thy Being.
[*Veils herself in her cloak, and goes lightly away.*

ROBERT (*without remarking her disappearance, lost in thought, to himself, Aside*).
Deeds?—I?—Yet, is renunciation not
An act?—Perhaps man's genuine aim and end?
Could, thus, ev'n I act, endlessly immured,
And live unfettered in my very chains? (*looking round.*)
Where is she?—Flown!—a light-winged morning dream!
I scarce can comprehend my bosom's fever,
Seven days since first I saw this vision gleam;—
My heart scarce holds this ecstasy supreme,
Unfelt before,—what was't?[1] But act, and question never;—
It was a dream—which, also, I'll renounce for ever!

CHARLOT (*enters quickly, laughing*).
Good even, Robert!

ROBERT.
How did'st thou pass in?

CHARLOT.
Why, by a leg of veal!

GOTTFRIED (*who wakes up at this interesting moment, yawning, as usual, widely*).
Wha—

CHARLOT.
From the priest,
'Twas stol'n for me by Elsie, and with it then
I bribed the guard.

[1] Robert, brought up from earliest childhood in quasi-monastic seclusion by Molay, has been aroused, by the sudden appearance in Cyprus of the beautiful Anchorite, to bewildering sensations, of which, while he feels the force, he has hardly had time to understand the meaning.— *Trans.*

ROBERT.
                Thou pleasant rogue!   Come give
A kiss! Without or mast or rudder sails
Thy pinnace, yet no less securely so
It clears the rocks!

            CHARLOT.
            I understand thee not.

        ROBERT.
Thou'st managed very well!

            CHARLOT.
                    But tell me, now,
How was it thou cam'st here?

            ROBERT.
                    An ancient tale
It is of yester-evening, aged almost
Of four-and-twenty hours, and can nowise
Repay thy hearing.—Tell me, rather, news
Of some sort, that the demon of ennui
Take not too fix'd possession of my poor head.

            CHARLOT.
Early to-morrow morning to Poictiers,
The Master sails with twenty knights, of whom
I'm one.

        ROBERT (*starting from his seat*).
    Thou liest!

            CHARLOT.
                Why, with the Draper, then,
I lie in company, who has already sent
On board all coats of mail and linen mantles,
With helmets, shields and lances.

        ROBERT (*deeply moved*).
                    And he leaves
Me here,—without his Robert he will go.—
The son may not accompany his father!

O trial worse than death!—Yet, she has taught—
(*Breaking off suddenly.*)
He has taught me to relinquish and renounce,
And, in a quicken'd sense of duty, left
His heaven behind with me! Good luck attend
Thee, Molay!

CHARLOT.
Poor, good Robert!—

GOTTFRIED (*who has at last arisen*).
We! To France? (*smiling feebly.*)
You're only joking!

CHARLOT.
By no means! 'Tis quite
Decided!

GOTTFRIED (*still hesitating and doubtful*).
Verily! Can it be?

CHARLOT.
This night,
Soon as appeared the cutter in the Roads,
Shone—(I was watcher on the Castle wall)
A light, by three o'clock,—in Molay's cell;
By five, the varlets hastened to and fro,
In every quarter, and at six o'clock
Went out the Grand-Commander, Draper, Marshal,
Treasurer, Standard-Bearer, Turcopolier,[1]
With all the other Ancient Knights[2] unto
The Master,—currently 'tis said, to hold
Exceptional Council.

---

[1] Commander of the Turcopols or half-caste light cavalry. Ducange derives the word from the Greek πωλος, a colt, thence offspring generally, of a Turkish parent, probably of Christian fathers. See "Notes and Queries," sixth series, April 4th, 1885, p. 277.—*Trans.*

[2] The dignitaries of the Temple Order were called "Ancient Knights," also "Good Men."

GOTTFRIED.
                    Early yesterday
They held already one.

                    CHARLOT.
                    What if they did!
The old stage-coach itself goes joltingly,
Because its horses now have got the staggers;
So there's no striding on with Spanish strut:
But rather break-neck haste with little speed.

                    ROBERT.
This must have made you very late at table,
Poor Charlot!

                    CHARLOT.
                    Not till one o'clock did they
Disperse. The meal was wholly spoilt. The Master
Came not himself to table. By half-past two,
Rode forth, full-speed, four hasty messengers,
Bound for the Bastion, Nikosia, Colossa,
Gastira. In the Castle's such a stir.
The busy people run against each other.
They're packing now the treasure, and they flit,
With varied play of colours to and fro,
Much like the mummers on Shrove-Tuesday, when
They lead the old Fool-mother by the nose.
The Grand-Commander shakes incessantly
His head; the Master is not to be seen,
Himself. Just think! From three this morn till now
(Soon sounds the bell for complines) he has sat
Not tasting bite or sup, dictating letters,
Holding deliberations, messengers
Despatching! 'Tis a marvel to me how
He weathers it, for this is the fourth night
He hath passed thus.

                    ROBERT (*pained, almost enryingly*).
                    His God within him keeps
Him up!

GOTTFRIED.
            Some news of weighty consequence
Must surely have arrived here.

                CHARLOT.
                        They all say,
A Bull has from the Holy Father come,
Wherein he cites us to him at Poictiers,
Safe-conduct guaranteeing. At midnight,
The Brief, they say, will be in Chapter read—
Also this night Poitou will be received,
And yet another, (*to Robert*) whom indeed you know!
'Tis he who with the pirate yesterday
Was taken.

                ROBERT.
                Tell me not of yesterday!
O God!

                GOTTFRIED.
        What? Who?

                CHARLOT.
                The stranger, the French Knight;
He is the son of Anjou's banished Duke.

                GOTTFRIED.
He?—What, so soon?

                CHARLOT.
                'Tis so indeed. The Master
Gave his consent reluctantly, they say—
But the Knight pleaded with such urgency,
He yielded to his prayer. He and Poitou
This coming midnight are to be received,
And in the early morning-tide—huzza!
We start for France!—Gottfried, thou also com'st
With us.

                GOTTFRIED.
        I am willing. For a gallant man
Is always complaisant. And come also,
The Brothers' Cook and Butler?

ROBERT.
                Parasite!

CHARLOT (to GOTTFRIED).
Thou Prince of gormandizers! Ay, they come.
            (To ROBERT, pointing to GOTTFRIED.)
He's found his proper niche! Come, foolish Robert,
Why so torment thyself? Thy father owns
Wealth, rank, authority.—My God! had I
Such power, such prospects, I'd be very glad
To lose my mantle. Then, light-hearted I
Would ramble through the world, until at length
I'd strike root in some castle of my own,
Take a young wife, go hunt the hart and roe,
And leave the Crescent, Cross, and Palestine
To God Almighty's guardianship.

                GOTTFRIED.
                    I too!—
Here's nothing but vexation. People say
We're necromancers,[1] and I think myself
There's something that is not quite orthodox
About our teraph-head.[2] God help us all!
'Tis well to keep one's sheep in pastures dry.

                ROBERT.
A spurious wisdom now you're babbling of,
The offspring of these frost-numbed latter times,
And, were it wisdom truly, oh! yet there floats
High o'er my heart a wholly different aim.
Be this a dream,—(I doubt it be scarce more)—
Yet ne'er would I exchange it for your Truth,
And for your joyless heaven. The Master may
Indeed have sacrificed himself for nought;
Yet would I sooner burn in that sweet dream
Than in the winter of your Truth I'd freeze.

---

[1] "They were commanded to extirpate magic and heresy. Lo! they are charged with studying the accursed cabalistical secrets of the Jews and the magic of the Paynim Saracens."—*Ivanhoe*, vol. iii., ch. v.—*Trans.*

[2] See note to p. 232, Act vi.—*Trans.*

GOTTFRIED.
Why, what do you mean?

ROBERT.
For you, nought; to myself
I am defining why it is my sighs
Are not a sound from empty organ-pipes,
And why I love one swan well-limnèd more
Than twenty living cuckoos.—Leave me in peace!

CHARLOT.
Original that thou art, and ever wert!

ROBERT.
In souls awake to love, and thought, and yearning,
A special ray of light, God-sent, is burning.
A man who manifests this ray from God
Stands out distinguished from the common clod.

CHARLOT.
Alas! the Grand-Commander!

COMMANDER HUGO (*comes hobbling in*).

COMMANDER (*to* GOTTFRIED *and* CHARLOT).
Now, now, now,
God mend it! You do well, good lads, to while
Poor Robert's time, your comrade. But now, go
And court your pillows for a little space,
For you must be in Chapter at midnight.
[*Exeunt* GOTTFRIED *and* CHARLOT.

COMMANDER (*fatigued, sitting down*).
Hast heard?—we go to-morrow morn to France?

ROBERT.
I have.

COMMANDER.
Wilt thou not drink a little draught
Of old wine of this country?[1] 'Tis allowed,—

---

[1] "The vines clothing the slope near Limasol produced the celebrated wine 'of the Commandery of the Temple.' The Knights, when they

For, to sick men and prisoners, the rules
Permit a cordial drink. 'Twas Moley's wish
To send it thee: but I begged it of him,
Because I fain would bring it thee myself.

ROBERT.
Herein I recognize both you and him.

COMMANDER.
Then drink to faithful brotherhood in life
And death! Come, drink. God mend it!

ROBERT.
    'Tis scarce meet
An outcast man should revel in the juice
Of golden grapes; but since he sends it me—(*he drinks.*)

COMMANDER.
That's right, my lad! (*Pauses,—during which he gazes on
  vacancy, lost in thought; then, looking up, as if
    recollecting himself.*)
    Ah, dost thou know? We sail
For France to-morrow.

ROBERT.
  You were saying so.

COMMANDER.
My poor old head becomes a little weak
At times.—This journey's strange!—It worries me,—
But since the Holy Father so decrees,
A Christian man must with good will obey.—
And hast thou slept well, through this night, dear youth?

ROBERT.
As a condemned angel might, who fell
With sudden shoot from his all beauteous heaven.

ceded the island to Guy de Lusignan, reserved the exquisite vineyards of Limasol, to establish there a Preceptory, where liberal potations were accredited to them, whence the proverb, Boire comme un Templier!"— *Hist. de St. Louis*, by De Villeneuve, vol. ii., p. 152.

" The wines known as *Commanderia* have always enjoyed a high reputation on the Continent."—*Handbook to Cyprus, Col. and Ind. Exhibition.*—*Trans.*

COMMANDER (*with increasing embarrassment, which he vainly tries to hide*).
Well, but—How think'st thou?—Come with us to France!

ROBERT.
You mock me! I am in the Church's ban.
My destiny is, Expulsion from the Order,
An endless dungeon.—Well,—'tis my desert!

COMMANDER.
Yes, that's all wrong!—Hark, Robert!—(No, I can't!)
Drink, then! What, thou—thou whom we need so much,
Of soldiers best,—thou, in this hole for life?—

ROBERT.
Right well *you* know the Order's rule severe.

COMMANDER.
'Tis true, God mend it!—Carping old man! I—
I,—now, thy health!
  [*Drinks from the flask, which* ROBERT, *after drinking, has replaced on the table; his hesitation is constantly becoming greater.*
  I—spoke—too hastily—
In truth. But thou, to be so heated too!—
Fie, Robert, fie! Why, what a fool wast thou!

ROBERT.
I was—a man—whom you've so often taught
To rate my honour higher than my life!

COMMANDER.
Thou'rt right, dear, youth! Yes, in good sooth, I have—
Truly I have. (*Half aside.*) Come, out with it, old man!
Why shame thee? If so madly thou could'st act,
Thou can'st but pay the forfeit! (*Aloud.*) Like a fool
I've borne me! Robert—Robert—come, forgive!—
  (*Relieved, and saying the rest with more composure.*)
Thank God! 'Tis out now—it oppressed me sore—

ROBERT (*deeply moved*).
My noble, honoured father! Oh, you heap
Hot burning coals upon my troubled head!
Oh, pardon, that for one brief space I broke
So sinfully through my sweet duty's bonds!

COMMANDER.
Yea, that was foolish!—

ROBERT.
                    Grant me once again
Your grace, and all my deepest wounds are healed.
                    [*With these words he falls on his knees
                    before the* COMMANDER, *and embraces
                    his knees.*

COMMANDER.
What dost thou there?—God mend it! Fie, stand up!—
A Templar kneels to no one but his God!
Fie, fie! stand up! (ROBERT *gets up.*) There's moisture
        in mine eyes,
Fie! Shame on thee, disgracing an old knight
With tears like women! Fie!—For shame, old man!

ROBERT (*embracing him*).
Oh, Father, let me kiss these tears away!

COMMANDER.
They are my first!—Leave me alone, bad Robert!
For if the people saw me, they would say:
" The old Commander now begins to dote;
He fought through eighty years, and lo, he weeps!"

ROBERT.
Oh could I set these first heroic tears
As pearls of price on that red Cross which now
Is lost to me for ever!—

COMMANDER.
                    'Tis not lost!—
No, no, God mend it! I will know no rest
But thou remainest in the Order!—

ROBERT.
                    Aye?—
And Odo Saint-Amand in prison died
For right and duty.   Did not you yourself
So tell me?—

COMMANDER.
              Go, boy, go!—Again thou mak'st
Me blush with shame (*embracing him*).
                This is not right of thee!—
Come to my heart!—It draws new warmth again,
God knows! from thine!   'Tis e'en as though thy youth
Infused new life into mine aged veins.—
                    [*Enter a* PURSUIVANT.

PURSUIVANT.
His Grace the Master sends me to command
Sir Robert to his presence.   (*To the* COMMANDER.)   He has asked
To see your Lordship also.

COMMANDER (*low to* ROBERT, *pointing to the* PURSUIVANT).
              I cannot
Confront him with these eyes so red!   Go thou,
Dear boy!   Things may be better yet,—but go!
                [*Exeunt* ROBERT *and the* PURSUIVANT.

COMMANDER.
But should he fall!—Oh father Hugo, spare!
Mete not strict justice to thy son's grey hair!
Oh shame on him who, when life's close draws nigh,
Must blush to think he fell from equity!

SCENE II.

(MOLAY'S *cell; in the centre a writing-table covered with papers.*) MOLAY (*sits behind the table, in the centre*). CHAPLAIN CYPRIANUS (*writing, on the right hand side*). Several Templar-Knights and Messengers. GREGER (*behind* MOLAY's *chair*).

MOLAY (*to a* KNIGHT).
This missive take to the Most Valorous
The Master of the Hospital (*gives him a letter*). I send
Him greeting, and I hope, on my return,
To visit him at Vesper-bread. [*Exit* KNIGHT.
(*To another* KNIGHT, *also giving him a letter.*)
This note
Thou'lt bear to Nikosia,[1] to the King
Of Cyprus, and deliver it unto
His Highness' very hands—mark that! and I
Commend to his good-will the Temple. Go!—
[*Exit* KNIGHT.
(*To another* KNIGHT *and three* MESSENGERS, *to whom he gives letters.*)
You four, in half an hour, will go on board
The barque from France which brought the mail last night,
And is prepar'd to sail. Soon as you land
(*To the* 1st MESSENGER)
Proceed to Paris, (*to the* 2nd) and thou to Ville-Dieu
En la Montagne, (*to the* 3rd) and thou to Montpellier.
And each of you will give the Brother Prior
His letter. (*To the* 1st.) And moreover greet from me
The illustrious Prior, Guido of Normandy;—
Tell him that I depend most certainly

[1] Guy de Lusignan, the first king, made Nicosia his capital city, a city embellished by magnificent palaces and churches. In the Cathedral of St. Sophia the Templars and Hospitallers had celebrated their Institutions, and there also most of the kings of Cyprus had been crowned.—*Trans.*

K

On finding him at Paris. (*To the* KNIGHT.) But do thou
Speed fast as on the pinions of the wind
To Poictiers; first to the Preceptor show
Thyself, and then, without delay, present
This letter to the Cardinal Promotor.—
Then, haply should the Holy Father grant
The foot-kiss to thee, tell him reverently
What's passing here, and that, in a few days,
Myself will come and kiss his Holiness' hands,
And with me, of the Templars sixty more.
Now go.   God prosper you!
   (*The* KNIGHT *and three* MESSENGERS *go.*)
(*To the* CHAPLAIN.) Is't ready, CHAPLAIN?

    CHAPLAIN (*writing*).
I am but colouring the initial letter.

    MOLAY.
Ah, let be,—give it here!
  (*Takes a paper out of his hands and reads it.*)[1]

GREGER (*who has hitherto been standing behind* MOLAY'S *chair,
  after a while addresses him timidly*).
       Will not your Grace
Be pleased to break your fast?—Collation 's ready.—

    MOLAY.
The brothers may partake.

   GREGER (*with gentle pleading*).
       But, gracious Sir!
Since two this morning you've sat fasting here!

   MOLAY (*with emotion*).
That troubles thee, poor Greger?—Let it pass!
Hast thou not still thy mother in Toulon?

    GREGER.
These seven years past she lies in Hospital—
The "Holy Ghost's"—She sent me word she fain

---

[1] "Mrs. Markham" says that De Molay could not read, in consequence of which he was led to affix his seal to a confession of crimes.—*Trans.*

Would see me once again before her end;—
But—

     MOLAY (*quickly*).
  So she shall! To Toulon thou shalt come
With me; there Brother Major-domo¹ I'll
Appoint thee, and thy mother then can live
With thee. What think'st? 'Twere not so well for me!

 GREGOR (*kissing his hand, unable to control his delight*).
God's Angel that you are! (*Recollecting himself and drawing
  back respectfully*) My gracious Lord!

    (*Enter a* PURSUIVANT.)

     PURSUIVANT.
The Grand-Commander and the Draper wait
Without: the Marshal also, as your Grace
Commanded. Also, Brother Robert waits
In the ante-chamber.

     MOLAY.
    Let the officials in—
Poor Robert must be patient yet awhile! [HERALD *goes.*

    (*Aside*).
I must be Master first; let feelings wait.

(*Enter the* MARSHAL *of the Order, the* PRECEPTOR, *the*
  DRAPER, *and the* PURSUIVANT.)

  MOLAY (*standing up, to the* PRECEPTOR).
Brother Preceptor! Has the frigate been
Got ready to make sail to-morrow morn
At early dawn, according to my orders?

     PRECEPTOR.
E'en now, sails bent, she lieth in the Roads.

    MOLAY (*to the same*).
The treasure, is't yet laden?

¹ So are named the Household Managers of the Country Preceptories
of the Order.
 The word is *Meier* (allied to the L. *major*, and the old German *meh*;
mehr). It is now obsolete in the sense of *Major-Domo.*—*Trans.*

PRECEPTOR.
                    Yes, the jewels,
The gold and silver vessels all are packed
Already—and the golden crown of Baph—

MOLAY.
Yes, that, of course, stays here.
            (*To the* MARSHAL *of the Order.*)
                    Are, Brother Marshal,
The lansquenets all equipped ?

MARSHAL.
                        They only wait
The bugle-call.
            MOLAY (*to the* DRAPER).
                    You would submit to me
The manifest of the baggage, Brother Draper.

        DRAPER (*handing him a paper*).
'Tis here.
            MOLAY (*reads*).
            One cuirass, helmet, sword, shield, lance,
And three surcoats; one Turkish club, and one
Doublet, two mantles, one fur coat and belt,[1]
Two shirts, two pair of breeches and two pair
Of hose, one paillasse, and one coverlet,
One sheet for each Knight—sixty Knights in all—
            (*Reckons it up mentally; then reads on.*)
Also for the Most-Valorous, mantles six,
And half-a-dozen shirts, and six pair hose.
    (*Glances over the paper, then stops reading, and says to the*
                        DRAPER)
Wherefore so much for me ?

DRAPER.
                    The custom is,
The Master takes thrice more than other Knights.

---

[1] Rule XXIII. "We have decreed in common council that no Brother shall wear skins or cloaks, or anything serving as a covering for the body in the winter, even a cassock made of skins, except they be the *skins of lambs or rams.*"—*Trans.*

MOLAY (*to the same*).
Stands it so in the Statute-book?

DRAPER.
Why, no,
But it is customary.

MOLAY.
Ancient use
Can ne'er shed lustre on a mean abuse.
Of old the Masters served their fellow-knights,
The essence surely of true Masterhood!
Not for their body's comfort, but to show
Example to their Brethren, did they wear
The Master-mantle; therefore will I too
So bear me, with God's help; and if on straw
Pallets the Brothers lie, no less can I,
Whom God appointed servant of them all.
(*Giving the paper back to the* DRAPER.)[1]
Your reckoning therefore change, and set me down
On equal terms with all the other Knights.—
Now, which of you has seen the Grand-Commander?

PURSUIVANT.
He has taken the Recipiends to Confession.

MOLAY (*to the* PURSUIVANT).
Thou'lt bring them to me after Sacrament.

CLAUS ROSNER (*Enters quickly, and hastily appproaches* MOLAY).

MOLAY (*Aside to him*).
Who'll close the vault?

---

[1] "The Draper was charged with the clothing department, and had to distribute garments, 'free from the suspicion of arrogance and superfluity,' to all the brethren. He is directed by the Rule to take especial care that the habits be neither too long nor too short, but properly measured for the wearer, with equal measure, and with brotherly regard, that the eye of the whisperer or the accuser may not presume to notice anything."—ADDISON, *Knights Templar*, ch. iii.—*Trans.*

CLAUS (*also Aside*).
          The Presbyter and I.

          MOLAY (*aloud to the* MARSHAL).
Is all made ready for the Chapter?

               MARSHAL.
                         Yes.

          MOLAY (*to the same*).
Who has the watch?

               MARSHAL..
          'Tis Charlot of Guyonne.

          MOLAY (*to the Knights*).
You are dismissed!   [*The officials of the Order go.*
          (*To the* PURSUIVANT.)
               Call Robert now to me!
                         [*Exit* PURSUIVANT.
(*Aside.*) Eternal Father, yet this bitter cup!
Shall I, yet one while, taste the cup of joy?

     (*Enter* ROBERT. *He remains standing at a distance with
                    bowed head.*)

          MOLAY (*turning to* ROBERT).
Draw nearer, Robert. (*To the* CHAPLAIN *and* GREGER.)
               You no doubt are tired?

               CHAPLAIN (*softly yawning*).
Ay, verily!

               MOLAY.
          Then sleep until midnight.

     GREGER (*Aside, and indicating* MOLAY).
And he, these six nights through, has slept no wink!—
               [*The* CHAPLAIN *and* GREGER *go.*

MOLAY (*to ROBERT, who is now alone with him, and has meanwhile come nearer*).
When I took thee, a little child of eight,
Into this Castle, and thy little sword
Girt on thee, and thy first lance gave to thee,
What vowed'st thou then to me?

ROBERT (*respectfully, and deeply moved*).
       Obedient ever,
To guide my ways by thy paternal voice.

MOLAY.
When, two years later, with my spear I slew
The wild boar, ere he rushed on thee, what then
Did'st swear to me?

ROBERT.
     To love thee as thy child,
And garner stores of joy for thine old age.

MOLAY.
And lastly, when I led thee, seven years since,
In that most solemn midnight of thy first
Induction, to the holy martyr Saint
Sebastian's shrine, what didst thou swear unto
The great World-master?

ROBERT (*eagerly*).
     Combat for the Right,
And law-enlightened daughter of the Right,
Immortal Freedom; self-surrender to
The inflexible control of iron Fate;
Obedience, self-denial, fidelity,[1]
Unswerving to my grave!—

MOLAY (*with solemn earnest.*)
      Robert!—this day

[1] "At the feet of my Superior I have laid down the right of self-action, the privilege of independence."—*Ireneus*, vol. ii., ch. ix.
"The Templar, serf all but in the name, can possess neither lands nor goods, and lives, moves, and breathes but at the will and pleasure of another."—*Ibid.*—*Trans.*

Stern Destiny reminds thee of thine oath.
The law's austerity expels thee forth
The Order—takes perhaps thy liberty
For ever from thee. Wilt thou, valiant Robert,
Practise renunciation, self-surrender?—

ROBERT.
I will—(*whilst he represses the springing tears*).
　　　Forgive my manhood's last revolt!
I will observe mine oath!

MOLAY.
　　　　　To-morrow morn
I go to France. Thou stayest in prison here—
What wilt thou do?

ROBERT.
　　　I will obey, renounce!

MOLAY.
The general Chapter yet may abrogate
Thy life-imprisonment, give thee freedom back;
Yet even this will scarcely profit thee,
For, as an outcast Templar-Knight, thou'lt be
A by-word to all people, high and low!—
And what, poor Robert, wilt thou turn to then?

ROBERT.
Proud in my rectitude, in deserts wild
I'll scorn the judgment of a foolish world!

MOLAY.
Should that be all thy brothers and mankind
May hope from thee?—Robert! 'twas thy desire
To garner joy for me!—

ROBERT.
　　　Can I do so?

MOLAY.
Robert! this day I tell thee once for all

Thou art a hero—Nay, far more than this,
Thou art a Man!—and 'tis my pride and 'tis
The solace of my age, thou'rt such through me.
My valiant Robert! only a weakling's strings
Lie shattered by the iron hand of Fate.
Fearless, the lofty-soul'd lays bare to fate
The harp which the Creator's hand has set
Within his bosom. Fate may strain the strings,
Yet not destroy the innermost accord
Of glorious tones, and soon the dissonance
Will melt again in purest harmony,
Because God's peace is breathing through the chords.
Strong-hearted Robert! Shall the stalwart man
Succumb, or rise triumphant from the dust?

ROBERT.

My Father!—

MOLAY.
                Shall the unalloyed true man
Be slave to his environments, or free?
Shall he not pluck from each storm-blast,—nay, more,—
From all the fond allurements of this life,
His purer Self?—The cosmos in his breast,
Part is't o' the elemental aggregate;
And shall not Nature's ferment, working there,
Upheave him also? Man! can'st thou succumb?—

ROBERT.

Yet there are moments—

MOLAY.
                    Yes, in truth there are,
But—God be thanked,—they're moments only, when
Subdued by mightier Nature's forces, man
Esteems his higher self a sport for waves.
In moments such as these, the Godhead shows
The distance yawning 'twixt itself and us.
And castigates the impious pride of man
Aspiring to equality, and casts

Him back into his natural nothingness.
In moments such as these the sage himself
Sinks into dust—the dust, whence he, too, sprang;
But soon uplifts himself and, purified,
Springs from the fateful crisis; and 'tis thus
The Holy Will proves its omnipotence.
Thou too, brave Robert, wilt rise up again!

ROBERT.
What can I do?

MOLAY.
            Be greater than thy fate,
Thy hater love; in works creative seek
The highest good, thy self-perfectionment.
Thou art the image of the Eternal One;
He, when mankind reviles Him, only smiles,
And round their huts creates a Paradise.
Wilt thou still, selfish, turn thee to the wilds?

ROBERT.
Humbled I bow before thy loftiness!

MOLAY.
That shalt thou not!—thou shalt me so surpass,
The best shall say hereafter: " good was Molay,
But Robert's a refulgence of the Highest!"
The Order, as I hope, will set thee free;
Thou knowest what Freedom's worth, and what she
      claims.—
Go back into the world!—not the great world;—
The world that's *thine!*—About thy father's castles
Thousands of men who are thy brethren, groan
'Neath heavy yoke of bondage;—set them free!—
By thine example, bring to nought the vile
Barbaric residue of Roman folly,
Which separates the free man from the serf,
As though all men had not one equal right,
By that first principle in-born to all,
Heart-glad to draw their breath in hope and love
And freedom!—Thou wilt be a feudal lord,

A lord of men! but they are likewise lords,
Because they're Men!' Show them the way to reach
Our Order's goal, which gleams victoriously
O'er death and tyranny; their father be,
And they most certainly will never dream
A warm paternal heart can beat the worse
If covered by no Cross; behold! all this
Thou canst do,—thou may'st do far more than I
Can compass. Oft, indeed, one man alone
Can more achieve than when combin'd with thousands;
For hard to influence are the wills of men,
And rarely does the better sense prevail.

     ROBERT.
Thou pourest oil into my bleeding wounds,
But hast thou balm to soothe the agony
Of leaving thee?

  MOLAY (*restraining his feelings with difficulty*).
     The balm for noble souls
Is, doing good. I,—to my sorrow too oft
Denied, O God!—this privilege by fate,
Commend it unto thee; it does but wait
Thy coming—go and meet it, happy man!
    (*Overcome by emotion.*)
And if some day, thou lean on thy wife's breast,
Thy children round thee, and a ray of joy,
Beamed from the world's Creator, thrill thy veins;
Then think of me who knew not father's joys,
Nor on flesh of his flesh might evermore
Repose his weary head, his bleeding breast!—

' It is commonly admitted that, while the accusation brought against
the Templars of Eastern heresies and the vilest criminality (how far
true or false it is hard to say) was the ostensible motor of their down-
fall, the actual cause of it was their immense wealth, which had be-
come a menace to the rest of the world. But this is an insufficient
explanation. They were obnoxious through having taken up the
cause of the people and the rights of humanity; and by being the
first to lift their voices against the iniquities attendant on feudalty,
and the despotism of Church and kings, they became antagonistic to the
ruling powers of Europe.— *Trans.*

ROBERT (*sinking on one knee before him in gentle grief*).
Give me thy blessing, Martyr!—

MOLAY (*with deepest, yet solemn emotion*).
May the Lord
Illumine thee with His most holy truth;
Exalt thee high, by hope and love and strength;
Refresh thy soul with joy and inmost peace.
And, when He to thy fathers gathers thee,
Leave thou this heritage unto thy sons,—
That when, one day,—we shall be sleeping then—
Bursts from our Temple the imprison'd flash,
And strikes asunder all the people's chains,
They shall already have rent in twain their own,
And stand array'd for battle, fully arm'd!

The PURSUIVANT (*comes up*).
The Grand-Commander, as you have desir'd,—

MOLAY.
Let him come in. [*Exit* PURSUIVANT.

MOLAY (to ROBERT, *who rises*).
Go hence in peace, my son!

ROBERT (*in unspeakable grief*).
And thou?—

MOLAY.
My own peace haply draweth nigh!—
[*Exeunt* ROBERT *and the* PURSUIVANT.

(*Enter* COMMANDER HUGO *from the other side.*)

MOLAY.
Has now the Chapter been convoked?

COMMANDER.
It has.

MOLAY.
My brave old comrade, wherefore art so sad?

COMMANDER (*pointing to the opposite door through which Robert went out*).
Was not that Robert, who went forth from thee?

MOLAY.
Ay, it was he.

COMMANDER.
I can't describe it, but
I feel that something snaps within my heart,
To see the young man thus.

MOLAY.
And is it not
Bad for me also?

COMMANDER.
Hast thou yet commands
For me?

MOLAY.
When have I ever laid commands
On my paternal friend?

COMMANDER.
Yet thou hast bid
Me hither.

MOLAY.
Sit thee down here by my side.
I hold here in my hand the instruction for
The Marshal, Brother Ulfo. Art thou now
Disposed to hear it?

COMMANDER.
My head's so confused!
Let be till morn!

MOLAY.
Because thou didst not wish
To take the Banner, I've trusted it to him.

COMMANDER.
'Twas that I asked of thee; for now, oh Molay,
My strength is drawing very near the grave!—

All's very strange with me to-day, God mend it!
Most marvellous! All that I do, I do
As though 'twere only for appearance' sake.
To-day there's such confusion—so much stir
As, usually, would quite have turned my head,
But now 'tis all the same to me! Erewhile,
I went down to the harbour where I saw
The rigging of the ship, and then, methought,
Some voice was whispering in my ear: "Behold,
That is thy winding sheet, and yonder bales
Thy coffin, that shall on the east-wind's wings
To-morrow to thy fathers carry thee."

MOLAY.
Then bide thou here! Enjoy well-earned repose,
And take the quiet ruling of the House.[1]

COMMANDER.
Nay! leave me not behind, comrade in arms!
I'll go with thee, and warm my aged limbs
Once more in that glad sun which has so oft
Burnish'd my bloody spear! and when in France,
Old Hugo calls me to his halls, lay thou
My body, in all its knightly panoply,
In oaken coffin; send it then to Aix
In Provence, that I there may sleep in peace
Sepultured in my fathers' tomb.

MOLAY.
          And who,
Hugo, will lay my body in a grave? (PURSUIVANT *comes up*.)

PURSUIVANT (*to* MOLAY).
The Acolytes—

COMMANDER.
     Now all go well with thee!
I go to try and rest a little while.   [*Goes.*

[1] Namely, the Templar-House (or Preceptory) at Limasol.

Frank of Poitou, Adalbert of Anjou appear, both dressed in black.[1]

MOLAY (*to* FRANK *and* ADALBERT).
Have ye your sins unburdened before God?
Have ye been purified, to firmly face
The stern probation, in this world your last?

FRANK.
We hope so, in the Father of all Grace.

MOLAY.
Are ye prepared all those things to renounce
Which heretofore have chained you down to earth?
The golden and irradiant crown of wealth,
Of pride the richly-tinted peacock plume,
The false, illusive jewel of self-will,
Yea, and no less, true valour's laurel-wreath,
The cord that bound you to your mother's heart,
Yea, e'en the perfumed myrtle-breath of Love,
The whole creation filled with all delight,
To bury in the Temple's open grave?

FRANK.
I am prepared.

ADALBERT.
I also!—Agnes sleeps
E'en now in her cool grave!

MOLAY.
Ye are but boys!
Consider what ye vow!—That moment when
This mantle falls upon your shoulders, rent
Are all your former ties, rent even those
High bonds by Nature hallowed,—severed all!
Ours are ye wholly: separated to
The Order, and betwixt you and those flowers

---
[1] "Behind them followed the Knight Companions of the Temple with a long train of Esquires, Pages, clad in black, aspirants to the honour of being one day Knights of the Order."—*Ivanhoe*, v. iii., ch. 13.
"The inferior officer of the Order wore black."—*Ivanhoe*, ch. 3.

Of earth, lies deep a terrible abyss!—
Turn back to them! Delicious is their scent,
And all around you lies God's earth outspread,
There also smiles on you His kindly sun,
And there right well ye can His children be!

FRANK.
I'll to the Highest devote my earthly fortune.

ADALBERT.
Mine's sleeping in the grave—my life is yours.

MOLAY.
Rush not unheeding to calamity.
Retreat is open still; soon 'twere too late.
Here persecution lies in wait for you,
And tribulation; worldly pleasure dies
Within these halls, desire of evil grows
More keen by its renouncement; should you here
Give place to it, you'll never rise again!
But e'en should you—I cannot guarantee it—
March forth as victor from the deadly fight;
E'en should you win the Order's highest prize,
The Saviour's glorious crown of martyrdom,
Suppose you that its thorns inflict no wound?
See, I am Master; painfully I won
The noblest prize you might by any means
Acquire,—this mantle. I am an old man,
I speak not vauntingly, I know full well
My strength is nought but merest impotence,
And God is mighty in me, who am weak;
Say I for my sake what I say to you?—
I say it to save your souls! Behold and see!
This linen mantle cost me six red wounds. (*baring his head*).
Feel on my skull and count them for yourselves.
One sword-cut would have surely cleft my head
Had not your father (*to* FRANK) warded off the blow.
(*To both.*) Yet little count I these, matched with those wounds
That pierced my inmost being, bleeding still;
The giving up of love, denial of that

Which Nature looks for from her children, oft
Has cost me many a strenuous conflict. Now
I have waxed old, and many of my wounds,
Are healed already by victorious Time;
Yet, other old men court repose in arms
Beloved, while I—I must turn night to day,
And ever restless strive, and ever fight
Against o'erwhelming force. With silvered hair,
I must bestir myself like a young man,
Must persecution undergo, and hate,
And may not rest nor ever taste the sweets
Of Love, the bright reduplicated Life.—
When sleep enfolds me in the late-drawn night,
No wife spreads me my couch; and when at last
The long sleep shall encompass me, mine eyes
No daughter tenderly shall close! Such then,
Am I, the Temple-Order's Master; One,
Elected o'er all others, called by Christ
To dominate o'er his Banner! And could ye
Hope e'en so much as that! Speak for yourselves!

FRANK.
I am resolved.

ADALBERT.
Me heavenly rest allures;
(*Aside.*) Soon will her spirit close my weary eyes.

MOLAY (*to* ADALBERT).
Rest seek'st thou here?—Almost thou mak'st me smile!
Look round thee! see from East, and West, and South,
Are darts directed to the Order's heart.
His sabre not alone the Saracen
Doth whet, to dye it with our blood, (*to both*) and yours;
The mighty powers of Christendom, beguiled
By futile dreams, are all against us ranged;
Around us rages on all sides the storm,
And round the Order's stronghold lift their crests
The hostile phalanxes, like waves upheaved.
Unless God's hand upholds us, we must fall;
And what will be your lot then, ye poor souls!

L

Where'er ye look, on every side, is death.
Turn back again! Thou, my good Adalbert,
Thou knowest the place where blooms thy sanctuary!

ADALBERT (*Aside*).
Yes—in the grave!—

MOLAY.
And thou, my dear Poiton!
Back to thy mother's loving arms return,
Thy sire's ancestral castle seek once more;
Support his hoary head, so battle-worn!

FRANK.
Himself he sent me here—I waver not!

ADALBERT.
For me remains no home but Heaven! I stay.

MOLAY.
Then stay!—But me accuse not before God!
For of this step of yours I solemnly
Absolve me of all consequence, and cast
Its burden on you!—You have made your choice,
I consecrate you to your destiny. (*Long solemn pause.*)
Prepare for the midnight solemnity;
When stroke of twelve comes booming from the tower,
Then will your lot be sealed. Depart and pray!
[FRANK *and* ADALBERT *go off.*

MOLAY (*Aside*).
Ay! there they go, the victims!
[*Suddenly rising from his seat.*
But by Heaven!
Almost I had forgotten! [*Calling after them.*
Adalbert!
(*To the* PURSUIVANT.)
Watch thou without, that we be not disturbed.
[*Exit* PURSUIVANT. ADALBERT *comes back.*

MOLAY (*to* ADALBERT, *as he opens a folding-door leading to the garden*).
First take leave of thy father!—

(PHILIP comes out of the garden, and is at the folding-door).

PHILIP (to ADALBERT, laying his hands on him).
                              Be a man!
May the Lord's strength be poured abundant o'er thee!
To God, who gave thee to me, I restore thee.
                              [Exit ADALBERT.

MOLAY (throwing wide open the folding-doors and looking out
    into the adjacent garden, which is already in twilight).
One freshening look on Nature's open face,
At close of this long, troublous day of pain!

PHILIP.
The evening's sultry.

MOLAY.
                Therefore the green earth
Pours forth for us sweet, wholesome fragrancy!
            [He inhales the air with a deep inspiration.
O, thanks be to thee for the breath of life,
All Bountiful! The spirits of the flowers
Return to thee, but as they pass, they cool
My burning temples tenderly; they love,
As I! (After a pause, during which his gaze has rested on
    the vale enamelled with flowers, to PHILIP.)
        To-morrow, when the stars revert
To gold, I shall be, Philip, far from thee!

PHILIP.
Now God forbid that I should thee forsake!
Past recognition grief has altered me;
Beard, raiment, ochre-staining will complete
My transformation, and I'll follow thee
Incognito, as one of thy armed men.
I'll stand as guardian angel by thy side,
I'll be thine escort to this island back,
And shouldst thou fall, I too will fall by thee!

MOLAY.
Into God's hand!

(*Pause, during which he gazes across the valley.*)
Yes, Brother, come with me!
Achilles and Patroclus once again;
Children we were, as children be our end.

PHILIP.
Strike hands on't. Life and death! (*Giving him his hand.*)

MOLAY (*joining hands*).
For life and death!

PHILIP.
One ship, one God, one credence, and one grave!

MOLAY.
Ay, and one myrtle from the Paradise
We planted in the darkness of midnight.
[*Embracing him.*
Now down fate's sultry highways we are going;
But o'er our steps faith's cooling airs are blowing.
Though round our ashes soon the winds shall play,
Sublime the seed we've sown will rise one day.
[*Whilst they are thus engrossed with one
another, EUDO passes by unseen, and
unobserved by them, with folded
hands.*

EUDO.
For, from dissolution
Springs life's evolution,
And Love wins a treasure of Love without measure.
[*Passes on.*

SCENE III.

Prison, as in Scene II. of Act III. Late in the evening. The scene is dimly lighted by a lamp standing on the table.

NOFFO,[1] CHAPLAIN CYPRIANUS, *stealing in, looking anxious.*

CHAPLAIN.
Have you yet mixed for him the electuary?

NOFFO.
So well that, if't be not the death of him,
He's ours entirely to command.

CHAPLAIN.
All praise
Be unto God, who such great things hath done
Through his unworthy servant, Cyprianus!

NOFFO.
Yet tell me, thou fat hulk! Deal honourably
For once!—say what it is they want of us?
Which coal is it thy Father Vincent would
Withdraw forth of the embers by our paws?

CHAPLAIN.
Why, look you, Noffodei, you're trustworthy;
And I may tell it you.

NOFFO.
Superfluous prologue!—
Friend, to the facts!—Thy gallows-tree's not yet built.

[1] "According to others, Noffo de Florentin, an apostate Templar, who had been condemned by the Grand Preceptor and Chapter of France to perpetual imprisonment for impiety and crime, made in his dungeon a voluntary confession of the sins and abominations charged against the Order."—ADDISON, *Knights Templars*, ch. ix.—*Trans.*

CHAPLAIN.
Of course a man of Father Vincent's rank
Writes not explicitly on every point;
But this much I am able to perceive,
Against the Order there are grave designs.
"*Deleatur illa rubra crux,*" he writes,
Where, writes he, "*supra clerum laicus.*"

NOFFO.
What does that mean?

CHAPLAIN.
        It means that the Red Cross
Must be expunged, according to God's will,
Because it is obstructive to the cowl.
Much has the Father heard, too, touching you,
And your shrewd wiles when to the Saracens
You made the fortress over. "Pity 'tis,"
He writes, "that this man should so vilely serve
The heathen's ends, for, with such gifts as God
Has lavished on him, he might be," writes he,
"A chosen vessel." Nor less well knows he
The impetuous man, the Prior. Of him he writes
"The resinous pine-knots serve to kindle fire;
Ply but the bellows well, he'll soon inflame,
And straight consume himself; and so 'twere best."

NOFFO.
What! that's the way of't, bellows? Well, go on!

CHAPLAIN.
Also the Father privately has given
Me charge to free from durance vile both you
And Brother Montfaucon, and so promote
Your welfare and dear Christendom's; and he waits
In Paris for you with a holy longing.
The note which as I hear you did but now
Read to the Prior, I drew up artfully
In Molay's name, and then to give the thing
A better colour I addressed it to
The Marshal of the Order. That part where

The Master plans the death of Heribert
Should, as I fain would think, remove the doubts
Which, by a culpable virtue's blinding spell,
This worldling from God's service still detain.
Could he be gained,—as sanguinely I hope
Through God and you he will be,—you will both
Escape to-day. The Frankish privateer,
Now anchored by the watch-tower to take in
Fresh water, as 'tis said—takes you on board,
And then—with God to France!

    Norro.
        Hear!—strike me dead!—
For by thy holy grey frock, brother Priest!
On Balaam's ass no mightier miracle
Was done, than this the Church has worked on thee.
The note thou'st forged with such dexterity
With Molay's signature stamped under it,
Wherein thou, clumsy devil else, couldst paint
The Master as a subtle fiend so deftly:
Who would have look'd for such skill'd artifice
In such a plethoric, thick, bald-pate?—Say now
Most eminent Cyprian, how doth holy Church
Contrive to raise up children for herself
From clods like thee?—

    Chaplain.
       You're jesting with your servant,
For know you not how mightily the Lord
Works in the weak? My patron said, (whose soul
God keep,) The humble monk is but a stone;
No higher and no lower he may lie
Than his place is: and if somewhat he be
Smaller than is the hole he's planted in,
The hole with mortar is filled up; but if
He's larger, his superfluous corners then
Must be chipped off: So superposed one stone
Lies on the other, no one knows aught of each;
And none returneth to his rock again
From whence they quarried him; one firmament
O'er-canopies alike the rough and smooth;

None seeth the foundation, and thus, or e'er
One looks for it, the holy Church is built.

NOFFO.
And twirls her weathercock to right and left
As veers the wind!

CHAPLAIN.
Silence, thou reckless railer!
Where is the Prior?

NOFFO (*pointing to the little door on the left*).
There in the little cell.

CHAPLAIN.
What said he when you read my letter to him?

NOFFO.
Said?—Naught! nor word nor sound escaped his lips.
First he stood still; then listened, as though he would
Seize with his ears each separate syllable.
Then shook his head, and pale as death clutched hard
The prison stool. At length to Heaven he raised
His eyes and clenched his fist; then ground his teeth,
Then threw his head so violently back
As though by dislocation of his throat
To burst his swollen veins, and separate
By violence chin from throat. So firm his feet
Were planted on the floor, not twenty men
Methinks could have dislodged one foot of his.
Then he began to laugh. I tell thee, Father,
Beelzebub will not more shrilly peal,
That day when he shall snatch thy sordid soul!
But soon this laugh to spell-bound stupor turn'd
And from his straining eyes two tears unchecked
Fell down, while foam stood on his parted lips.
I gently laid my hand on his clenched fist,
And undesignedly he struck me with't
So rude a blow I could not see nor hear;
Then stood he still, nor budged for half an hour;
Then heaved a sigh a fathom deep, which soon
Was followed by loud cries, and staggering like

A drunken man, he sought with tottering steps
The chamber, where he sank upon the couch.

CHAPLAIN.
And sleeps?

NOFFO.
    And sleeps!—well! if we call that "sleep."
I rather would keep watch in purgatory,—
Come in thyself and see.
    [*Taking the lamp from the table, he leads
    the* CHAPLAIN *to the little door on the
    left, which he opens slowly.*]
    Can'st make him out
By the lamp's glimmer?—See, open stand his eyes;
And yet I'd wager he would nothing see
Albeit the devil himself stood there and grinned.
    [*Looking more closely into the cell and
    searching round with his eyes.*]
But look! Is't fancy?—Verily methinks
There glitters round him vaporously a light—

CHAPLAIN.
No, 'tis the lamp-light's shining, and we know
It is the property of light to shine!

NOFFO.
May be!

CHAPLAIN (*also peering into the cell*).
    Look, how he's crumpling that fair sheet
Of paper!—all those well-formed characters!

NOFFO.
That is the letter which he grips, as though
'Twere rooted in his palm. He knits his brow,
He stirs—hark!—hush!—what words are these he mutters?

CHAPLAIN.
Nought hear I!

NOFFO.
    Hark! Now dost thou nothing hear?

CHAPLAIN *(listening).*
I hear!—He murmurs somewhat of "revenge"
And "sweet" I think,—and so forth.

NOFFO.
Ay! that's it!
'Tis the old burden of a horrid song
That haunts his head, unresting like a ghost.
See there again! he shudders, he gets up!
Come out, come out, if we would keep whole skins.
The man is raving—he'll lay hold on us.
  [*He hurries to the front dragging the* CHAPLAIN
  with him, and sets the lamp on the table.
  PRIOR HERIBERT *comes wildly rushing
  through the door on the left.*

PRIOR.
Who's moving yonder?—(*wearily to the* CHAPLAIN).
Chaplain, is it you?
Methinks I've dreamt a fearful dream.

CHAPLAIN.
How so,
My worthy Prior?

PRIOR.
Look you!—I dreamt there was
A letter most malignant and most black,
Most devilish and accurst—but sure 'twas naught
But dreams! [*The letter he was holding falls from his hands.*

CHAPLAIN.
E'en now, you are letting fall the note—

PRIOR (*turning upon him*).
What, thou vile caitiff! Would'st thou play on me
More of thy scoundrel tricks?—Down with thee, cur!
  [*He seizes the* CHAPLAIN, *who shrinks terrified.*

NOFFO (*unloosing him*).
Prior, are you possessed? At such a time,
With all our lives at stake?—

PRIOR (*to* NOFFO).
Ay!—thanks, my friend!

Thanks, rascal-friend, for timely warning me.
(*Softened, to the* CHAPLAIN.)
Hear me, your Reverence!—Some time ago—
About eight days, I think—did Noffodei
Send me a curious letter, which gave me much
Amusement. I would like to hear it read
A second time. My dear friend, read it me!—

CHAPLAIN.

With pleasure! only I fear—

PRIOR.

I' the devil's name, read!

CHAPLAIN (*reads with every sign of fear, at the same time keeping sharp watch on the* PRIOR, *with stolen glances*).
"Private instruction for the Brother Marshal.
I must, beloved Brother, ere I go,
Unfold to you the secret of my soul.
Repeat no word of it, upon your life!
You know the arrogant Prior Montfaucon,
You know what has occured 'twixt him and me.
'Tis true he lieth in prison, but the snake
Is only scotched, it keeps its venom still,
And dangerously will raise its head again
Unless we tread it down. Dear Brother, while
He still draws breath, Molay sleeps not secure.
The Chapter, Brother, is favourable to him.
Should one decree be in his favour passed,
He'll start up stronger than he ever was.
This needeth haste!—To-morrow, Brother, I go,
The following day will set the prisoner free.
Let him be freed—you mark me!—from the bonds
Of prison and of life—and without blood."

PRIOR.

The thing's impossible!—Give me the note!
(*He snatches it from the* CHAPLAIN'S *hands and looks at it.*

NOFFO.

You cannot read!

PRIOR.
True—true—My head!—
[*Gives the letter back to the* CHAPLAIN.
Go on!

CHAPLAIN (*reading on*).
"Of prison and of life—and without blood.—
A little hemlock with his cabbage mixed,
A little hole the depth of seven ells;
So sleeps he peacefully, and so do we.—
Farewell! And if this be a sin,—I take
The burden of it on my shoulders!—MOLAY."

PRIOR (*breaking into the hottest rage*).
Oh, lend to me thy lightnings, Heaven! O Hell,
Give me thy flames! (*To* NOFFO) Tell me, thou scoundrel, how
Thy hands obtained this gallows-reeking letter?

NOFFO.
Must I repeat it ten times? (*Pointing to the* CHAPLAIN.)
He can tell!—

CHAPLAIN.
When Molay was dictating, yesterday,
Despatches to me, he stopped short and looked
Me shrewdly in the face; "Chaplain," said he,
"You're a true man. Can you a secret keep?"
And I, all unsuspecting, answer made,
"Most Valorous, sure my bosom is no echo:
'Tis but a shrine which faithfully conceals
All you repose within it," I said: thereon,
Many injurious things he said of you,
And bade me, by mine oath and by Christ's wounds,
Divulge them never; and when I'd promised him,
He bade me that disgraceful note inscribe.
Six times I longed to throw in his vile face
The pen, but used discretion, you to save.
I wrote the note and handed it to Molay;
But during the brief space when he was gone
To lunch, I seized my opportunity,
Transcribed the note, and thrust into my hood

The copy I had made for you; you being
Asleep,—I gave to faithful Nossedei
The draft, which he delivered, I hear, to you.
(*Aside*) Thank God, that now I've got well through the task
Set me by Father Vincent!—

      Norro.
        Well, Prior, what
Say you?

  Prior (*who hitherto has stood stiff with rage, now breaking
     loose upon the* Chaplain).
      Priest! If thou liest, yea, if thou liest,—
Then God have mercy on thee!—

     Chaplain (*trembling*).
         Surely as
Christ's living waters freely flow for me!
This is pure truth which I make known to you.

    Norro (*to the* Chaplain).
The letter's gone?

      Chaplain.
    Delivered to the Marshal.

   Norro (*aloud to the* Chaplain).
Now, Chaplain, best of friends! (*Quickly and aside to the same.*)
       You must be quick!
He'll break loose from our toils if he reflect.
(*Aloud*) Tell us, friend Chaplain, what have we to do?

      Chaplain.
All has been carefully provided for.
This night upon the stroke of twelve there'll be
Reception in the Chapter. The Brothers all
Will there assemble; at which time will creep
Beneath your window, and call "Cuckoo" twice,
The Sexton Otto, in whom you may confide.
But ere he come, you'll with this crowbar raise
    [*Draws a crowbar from under his robe, and
      gives it to* Norro.

The lattice, and precautionally don
These cowls.
   [*Draws out two monks' cowls and gives them to the same.*
    Here!—They are consecrated robes,
And so your shield 'gainst evil chance. Then he
Calls "Cuckoo," and the third time he shall call
You'll let yourselves descend by these two cords.
      [*Gives them also to* NOFFO.
He has the key that opes the garden-door:
And to the bastion will conduct you through it,
Where there's a subterranean way, unknown
Save to the Master, and some few of the Elders;
A small door shuts it in, the key of which
I, subtly, from the Master have purloined.
With this key Otto will unlock the door,
And through the passage to the end of it
Will lead you safely; then he'll part from you,
And you keep to the left, as far as to
The Chapel of our dear Lady of the Sea.
Then comes, you know, a little stretch of forest,
And then, at once, the harbour. At the watch-tower,
One, clad in mantle blue, will stand and say
To you, "It rains." Then you shall answer him,
"Sets the wind fair to-day?" He'll bring you then
On board a ship, which came, express, from France
To take you off. And she, ere morning break,
Will stand to sea, and with a favouring wind,
You'll be at Calais after seven days.

  NOFFO (*feigning to be overwhelmed with joy*).
Chaplain, thou'rt born to be a Cardinal!

    CHAPLAIN.
The skipper will provide you money. When
You land in France, make haste without delay
To Paris; at Saint Augustine's abbey ask
For Father Vincent; give to him this note [*Gives it to* NOFFO.
And trust the rest to him and our dear Lady!—

   NOFFO (*to the* PRIOR).
Comrade! thou hear'st?

PRIOR.
                    Comrade? Well be it so, Hell
Has made us brothers. (*To the* CHAPLAIN) Priest, thy hand
    upon it!
(*To* NUFFO) Here, Noffodei, thy hand upon it!—I'm yours!—
I'll go to France, the Pope, the King himself.
Ha! I'd not murder him, foul hypocrite!
Ah, no! but I will slowly torture him,
And when the torment's gnawing at his life,
I'll taunt him with this grisly cry: "Behold
The serpent's head!" [*Seizing one of the cowls from the table.*
                    Give me the cowl! So! Now
I'm ready for the journey.

            CHAPLAIN (*to the* PRIOR).
                    Fare you well,
Dear friend, soon Master of the Order!—Now
I must be gone. Soon tolls the Chapter-bell.
E'en now the Acolytes wend towards the Church.
Adieu!—

                    PRIOR.
        Adieu! We meet again, unfailing,
E'en now the owl's prophetic death-songs wailing;
The great exploit begins at midnight, when
The fiend and vengeance watch o'er blindfold men.
                            [*Exit* CHAPLAIN.
    (*Curtain falls.*)

ACT V.

SCENE I.

Midnight. Interior of the Church of the Order. Behind is a far perspective of altars and Gothic pillars. Towards the right side of the foreground, a small Chapel, and in it an altar with the statue of St. Sebastian. The scene is dimly lighted by a lamp hanging in front of the altar.

FRANK OF BRIENNE
(Clad entirely in white, without doublet and mantle).

HERE must I wait?—How from the lofty dome
 Each footstep that I take reverberates down
E'en to the cavernous dwellings of the dead,—
Safe home of hearts that suffer pain no more!—
Mine only beats—(I almost hear it throb)
In this terrific stillness of the tomb;
For those who lie beneath now breathe no more;
They rest in dissolution's long, long sleep! (*Pause.*)
Hark! something moves!—'tis but the pendulum
That sounds with hollow beat from the tower-clock.
Its stroke is calm, yet never ceasing, e'en
Like Fate. Beneath it hearts may break or glow
Exultant; neither troubles it! One, two,
Three, four, five, six—like blows which iron death
Deals with his hammer on our hearts, thereby
To stamp on them remembrance of the path
From which there is no possible return!—
Me will he lead to light's eternal source,
Or draw me downward to the dark abyss?
           [*Pause. The tower-clock strikes twice.*
Half-past eleven!—one only half-hour more,

And twelve strikes from the tower; cast thenceforth is
The lot, and rent the links with human kind!
Is this chill shiver coursing through my bosom,
So clammy-cold, their valediction?—Hold!—
The church doors clang together gloomily,
The floor re-echoes with an iron tramp!
Is this perhaps death's footfall entering?
  (*A man clad in black armour from head to foot,*[1] *with
      closed visor, comes up.*)

ARMED MAN.
  Pray!—(FRANK *kneels down.*)

Disrobe thyself!
  (*He strips him down to the girdle, and raises him up.*
  Look downwards!—Follow me!
  (*He leads him to a trap-door, on the left,
      in the background, then goes down
      first.* FRANK *follows him, whereupon
      the door closes.*

Enter ADALBERT (*clad like* FRANK, *groping in the
    darkness*).
Was I not told to wait for the Unknown
At St. Sebastian's altar? Yes! I think
'Twas so; but this thick pall of darkness veils
The figures—(*stepping to the altar*). Here is the fifth pillar!
  Yes,
The Saint is there. The mild gleam of the lamp
Falls softly on the youth's half swooning gaze!
O, here's no work of Saracenic lance!
These are the pangs of love, which, scorching, pierced
Thy bleeding heart, companion of my pain!
O mine own Agnes!—Doth perchance thy shade
Look down upon me in this solemn hour?
In yonder moonbeam haply dost thou float,
Which shimmers through those painted window-panes,
And in the cloister's darkness vanishes?—
Or else, behind those arrows dost thou bide
Which loom on me so black, so ominously,
As on the Present, loom horrors of the Past,

[1] Namely, the Presbyter of the Order.

And hide from me thy pure and lovely form
That thy pale countenance dismay me not?
Hide not thyself from sight of thy belov'd
Spirit of my Agnes! Thou affright'st me not!—
Hark! Is not someone rustling even now?—
Father, is't you?

PHILIP (*who comes in wildly and hurriedly*).
     Yes, Adalbert. But time
Is precious! Come with me, my only son!

ADALBERT.
What would you, Father, now, in such an hour?

PHILIP.
If not this hour, my son, then nevermore!
   (*Leading* ADALBERT *to the altar.*)
Approach! Thou knowest this youth, and who he is?

ADALBERT.
'Tis St. Sebastian!

PHILIP.
    As he would not yield,
And disavow his faith, a tyrant's will
Transpierced him with these arrows. Tyranny
Has likewise bleached this head (*pointing to his own*), a
  despot's rage
Has also ploughed with many deep-cut lines
These furrows on thy father's countenance!
My son! my firstborn, and my only child!
In this supreme, in this most awful hour,
I here adjure thee—do as I command!

ADALBERT.
What you command is right, and I concur!

PHILIP.
Then swear to me in this tremendous hour—
By this thy father's head made early grey,
Thy mother's terror-stricken death of pain,

And by the blighted blossom of thine Agnes,—
Eternal, bloody, unrelenting hate
To Tyranny, these victims' murderer!

ADALBERT.
There spoke the eternal Nemesis through thee!
Yes! Agnes' funeral torch shall bloodily
Burn in the tyrant's heart—and that I swear!

PHILIP (*with ever-increasing excitement*).
And if thou violate this awful oath,
If with the tyrant thou be reconciled,
If golden chains and gifts of his, his prayers,
Or his death-rattle even, disarm thine hand—
The avenger's hand—shall then this hair, too soon
Turned grey, the agonizing cry of her
Who bore thee, shall thine Agnes' withered bloom
Accuse thee, all, before the Eternal's throne?

ADALBERT.
So shall they, if I ever break my vow.

PHILIP.
Be strong then!
                [*Looking up and hastily shrinking, whilst
                    he peers around.*
                Was not that his lightning flash?
Farewell!—The doors are changing even now,
I hear the footfall of the Terrible One!—
Remember always this midnight, and me!   [*Exit hastily.*

ADALBERT (*alone*).
Yes, grey head, sent me, at the Lord's behest,
To wake to action out of abject sleep;
I will remember thee and this midnight
Avenged shall be my Agnes' spirit!

(Another MAN IN ARMOUR,[1] *equipped precisely like
the first*).

[1] Namely, Claus Rösner.

MAN IN ARMOUR.
Pray! [ADALBERT *kneels down.*
Disrobe thyself! [*Strips to the girdle and raises him up.*
Look downwards!—Follow me!
[*Leads him to the background, on the right, to another trap-door, into which he descends first, like the former man in armour, and which closes as soon as* ADALBERT *has followed him.*

SCENE II.

Crypt of the Templars under the Church. The scene is lighted only by a lamp, suspended from the vaulting. Around are tombstones of deceased knights, engraved with crosses and bones of dead men. In the background, two colossal skeletons, holding up a large white book marked with a red cross, from the under edge of which hangs a long black curtain. The book, of which only the cover is visible, has an inscription in black cipher. The right-hand skeleton holds erect in its right hand, a naked sword; that on the left holds, in its left hand, a Palm-branch pointing downwards. On the right side of the foreground a black coffin stands open: on the left is a similar one, with the corpse of a Templar-Knight in full panoply of the Order; on both coffins are inscriptions in white cipher. On both sides, nearer to the background, are visible the lowest steps of the flights of stairs, which lead up to the Church of the Order, above the vault the First ARMED MAN (*with naked sword*) and FRANK. *Afterwards, the Second* ARMED MAN *and* ADALBERT.

ARMED MAN.
The trial's ended!—Forth to the reception!

Second ARMED MAN (*not visible as yet; above, on the right-hand stairs*).
Terrible One! Is the tomb open?

HIDDEN VOICE.
Yes!

Second ARMED MAN (*after a pause, shows himself on the right-hand stairs*).
May he behold the fathers' tomb?

HIDDEN VOICE.
He may!
[*Second ARMED MAN, with naked sword, leads ADALBERT carefully down the steps on the right.*

ARMED MAN (*to ADALBERT*).
Do not look up!—Thy life shall pay for it else!
[*Leads him to the open coffin.*
What dost thou see?

ADALBERT.
A coffin, open, void.

ARMED MAN.
That is the house that shall be thine to-morrow!
Canst read the inscription on the coffin?

ADALBERT.
No.

ARMED MAN.
Its purport is: "The wage of sin is death!"
[*Leading him to the opposite coffin, wherein lies the corpse.*
Do not look up—thy life would pay for't; follow!
[*Shows him the coffin.*
What dost thou see?

ADALBERT.
A coffin with a corpse.

ARMED MAN.
To-morrow thou shalt be like this thy brother!
Canst read the inscription on the coffin?

ADALBERT.
No.

ARMED MAN.
'Tis "Dissolution is the name of Life."
Look up, go forward now. Examine and act!
> [*Pushes him towards the background of the Stage.*

ADALBERT (*observing the book*).
Ha, what is this? The book of Ordination?
> (*Drawing nearer to it.*)

The inscription on the cover seems legible.
(*Reads it.*) "Knock four times on the floor,
Thou thy belov'd shalt see."
Ha! is it possible? Shall I look on thee,
Mine Agnes glorified? (*hastily approaching the book*).
Come to my heart!
> (*Saying the following words, he stamps four times with his foot upon the floor.*)

One, two, three, four!
> [*The curtain hanging from the book, rolls rapidly up, so as to cover it. A colossal demon's head appears between the two skeletons; its countenance is horrible; it is gilt, has on a huge golden crown, a heart of the same on its brow, rolling fiery eyes, serpents instead of hair, golden chains round its neck, which is visible as far as the breast, and a golden cross (but without crucifix) projecting over the right shoulder, and seeming to crush him down. The whole bust rests on four gilt dragon-feet. At sight of it* ADALBERT *starts back full of horror and cries:*)

Jesu! Maria! Joseph!

ARMED MAN.
Terrible One! May his ears hear it?

HIDDEN VOICE.
                    Yes!—

ARMED MAN.
    [*Touches with his sword the rolled-up
    covering. It rolls down in front of
    the demon-head, which is thus with-
    drawn from sight, and above it, as
    before, appears the book, but now
    opened, with immense white leaves,
    and red characters. The ARMED
    MAN pointing constantly to the book
    with his sword, and turning the leaves
    with it, says to ADALBERT, who is
    standing on the other side of the book,
    more towards the foreground.*

Now hear the history of the fallen Master!
    [*He reads from the book as follows, stand-
    ing not in front of it, but sideways at
    a few paces distance, and as he reads,
    turning the leaves of the book with
    his sword.*

And when the first foundation-stone was planted
The Lord called forth the Master, Baphometus,
And said to him, "Complete my Temple's building!"
But in his secret heart the Master reasoned:
What profiteth it me to build the Temple?
And took the stone, and built himself a dwelling;
And whatsoever stone was left thereover
He bartered it for paltry gold and silver;
But after forty moons, the Master-builder
Met him with "Where's my Temple, Baphometus?"
"My own house, I was forced to build," he answered,
"Have patience yet for forty weeks, I pray thee.
Then came the Lord when forty weeks were over,
And asked, "Where is my Temple, Baphometus?"
He said, "Behold, there lacks me stone for building,"
(Yet he for paltry gold the stone had bartered;)
"And therefore yet for forty days have patience."
To him, returning forty days thereafter,
The Lord cried, "Where's my Temple, Baphometus?"

And weighed down was his soul as by a mill-stone,
To have for paltry gold the Lord defrauded.
But yet the fiend to further evil drove him;
And so he cried: "Yet forty hours accord me!"
And when the forty hours were passed and over,
The Lord upon him in his wrath descended,
And threatening cried, "My Temple, Baphometus!"
Then fell he on his face and begged for mercy,
All trembling; but the Master-builder answered:
"Because with empty lies thou hast deceived me,
And for a purse of paltry gold hast bartered
My stone which I had lent thee for my Temple,
Behold! now also I will cast thee from me,
And will by Mammon's very self chastize thee,
Until one day there shall arise to save thee,
Sprung from thine own seed, one that shall deliver."
Then took the Lord the purse filled with gold pieces,
And shook into a crucible the pieces;
Then set the crucible in burning sunlight,
Till to a liquid mass the gold was molten;
Then in the crucible he dipped one finger
And stretched the finger out to Baphometus,
His brow, his chin, his right and left cheeks daubing
With molten gold, the gold his purse had yielded.
Then changed in countenance was Baphometus,
Like flames of fire his lurid eyes were rolling,
His nose became a hookèd beak of vulture,
His tongue from out his throat protruded bleeding,
The flesh that clothed his hollow cheek was shrunken,
And from his hair came actual serpents growing,
And from the serpents sprouted horns of devils.
The Lord then raised his gold-anointed finger,
And pressed it on the heart of Baphometus;
Then was his heart set bleeding and was shrivelled,
And all his limbs were bleeding and were shrivelled,
And dropped away, first one and then the other,
And last of all the whole trunk sank in ashes;
The head alone continued gilt and living,
And where the trunk was, sprouted feet of dragons,
Which blasted from the earth all living juices;
The bleeding heart which even as he touched it,

Was turned to gold, the Lord from the floor lifted,
And set it in the fallen outcast's forehead;
The gold yet in the crucible he fashioned
Into a red-hot kingly crown, and pressed it
Down on his snaky hair until the circlet
Burnt to the very bone. Gold chains he twisted
Tight round his neck, well nigh to strangulation;
And that still in the melting-pot remaining,
Upon the ground he poured it, cruciform-wise,
So that it formed a Cross, which he uplifting
Upon his back laid, and to earth so bent him
He could not lift his head again for ever.
Two Deaths he set as sentinels beside him:
One, Death of Life, and Death of Hope the other;
He cannot see the first's sword, yet it smites him,
But sees the other's palm, yet it evades him;
So languishes the outcast Baphometus,
Through years four thousand and moons four and forty,
Till once a Saviour from his own seed risen
Shall come at last, redeem him and deliver.
(*To* ADALBERT.)   That is the story of the fallen Master!
                 [*With the point of his sword he touches
                 the curtain, and it rolls up over the
                 bust as before, so that the demon-
                 head beneath it becomes again visible
                 as before.*

        ADALBERT (*looking at the head*).
How horrible a shape!

        THE HEAD (*in hollow tones*).
          Deliver me!

        ARMED MAN.
Terrible One, say shall the work begin?

        HIDDEN VOICE.
Yes!

        ARMED MAN (*to* ADALBERT).
Take his throatlet off! (*pointing to the head*).

ADALBERT.
I may not dare!

THE HEAD (*whose tone grows more piteous*).
Deliver me!

ADALBERT (*taking the gold chains off him*).
Alas, thou poor apostate!

ARMED MAN.
Take off his crown!

ADALBERT.
It seems so dire a weight!

ARMED MAN.
Thou need'st but touch it, and it will be light.

ADALBERT (*after he has taken off the Crown and thrown it on the ground as he did the chains*).
'Tis done!—

ARMED MAN.
Now take off from his brow the heart
Of gold!

ADALBERT.
Ah me! it seems to burn.

ARMED MAN.
Thou err'st,
'Tis colder far than ice.

ADALBERT (*taking the heart from the forehead*).
Ah!—freezing cold!

ARMED MAN.
The cross take from his back. Throw it on the ground!

ADALBERT.
The token of my Saviour's martyrdom?—

THE HEAD.
Deliver, oh, deliver me!

ARMED MAN.
                Not this
Thy Master's cross, the bloody cross; this is
Only its counterfeit.   Throw it on the ground!

    ADALBERT (*taking it from the boat, and softly
                laying it on the floor*).
The cross of my dear Lord, who died for me!—

            ARMED MAN.
Our faith is not in One Who once has died:
We but believe in One who surely lives,
And never died!—Obey and question not.
Tread o'er it as you go!

            ADALBERT.
                Oh spare me this!

    ARMED MAN (*threatening him with the sword*).
Tread over it.

            ADALBERT.
With shuddering I obey!
            [*Treads over it, and looks up to* The Head,
                *which raises itself as if freed from a
                heavy burden.*
Ah, with what sensible relief this shape
Looks up and rolls its eyes!

            ARMED MAN.
                    Him whom thou hast
Been wont to serve, deny!—

            ADALBERT.
                    Deny the Lord
My God?—

            ARMED MAN.
        Nay, not thy God—the world's
False God!—Deny or (*approaching him with the sword*)
    perish!

ADALBERT (*trembling*).
I deny!

ARMED MAN (*pointing to the demon-head with his sword*).
Approach the fallen one—and kiss his lips!

ADALBERT (*with uttermost horror*).
For God's sake, no! for all my blood runs cold
At the bare aspect of his gory mouth.

ARMED MAN.
He is thy twin-brother,—therefore kiss thou him!

ADALBERT.
No,—rather death!

THE HEAD (*with soft beseeching tone*).
Deliverance, Adalbert!—

ADALBERT.
Thy tone is soft, 'tis like my Agnes' voice!
(*Resolved.*) I will deliver thee!—Oh radiant maid!
Be thou my help, lest Nature's vital power
Succumb to the drear horror of this deed!
[*After yet a few gestures of loathing, he at last steps quickly to* The Demon-Head *and embraces it.*

THE HEAD.
I thank thee!
[*At this moment* The Head, *carrying with it* ADALBERT *embracing him, the skeleton, and the book, sinks beneath the floor.*

ADALBERT.
Save me, I am sinking! Help!

ARMED MAN (*stretching his arm into the opening*).
Climb up, my Brother, on thy Brother's arm!
[*He pulls out* ADALBERT, *who clambers out by his arm.*

ADALBERT.

Thank, oh thank God!—My hair still stands on end!
(*Pointing to the still open cavity from which he came up.*)
What dreadful darkness! Ha! I am drenched with blood!

ARMED MAN.

Listen!

[*The lamp suspended from the Dome goes out; in the background, where lately stood the skeletons and The Demon's Head, there appears above, in a coloured transparency, a decapitated head and a sword lying in a trencher;*[1] *from the spot where it appears, the following words sound forth,*

Redemption springs from Blood and Darkness!

[*The apparition goes slowly to one side, while* ADALBERT *is speaking, and then disappears.*

ADALBERT.

See I aright?—Whose is the bloody head?
(*Hastening towards it.*) Depart not yet! 'Tis e'en already gone!

ARMED MAN.

'Tis the Baptiser, who with fire baptises!
From his blood's fountain the red Cross arose,
The true Cross of the Saviour, and our sign.

[*Points with his sword towards the middle of the background, where on the very spot where The Head had been seen appears a transparently-painted red Cross, having the attributes which he proceeds to enumerate.*

And from the Cross shoot upwards unto Heaven
The solstice, and the roses and the palms.

[*He swings his sword.*

Close up thy portals, Heaven! [*The apparition vanishes.*

---

[1] Apparently the head of John the Baptist, whose name Molay in the next scene couples with those of God and Our Lady.—*Trans.*

                    Brood, dark midnight!
                 [*The Stage becomes completely dark.*
The trial's ended. Forth to the reception!
                 [*He leads* ADALBERT *to the left-hand steps,
                 which they ascend together.*

NOTE.—On this Scene, Carlyle thus comments: "How much of this mummery is copied from the actual practice of the Templars we know not with certainty: nor what precisely either they or Werner intended, by this marvellous story of the Fallen Master, to shadow forth. At first view one might take it for an allegory, couched in Masonic language,—and truly no flattering allegory,—of the Catholic Church: and this trampling on the Cross, which is said to have been actually enjoined on every Templar at his initiation, to be a type of his secret behest to undermine that Institution, and redeem the Spirit of Religion from the state of thraldom and distortion, where it was then held. It is known at least, and was well known to Werner, that the heads of the Templars entertained views, both on religion and politics, which they did not think meet for communicating to their age, and only imparted by degrees, and under mysterious adumbrations, to the wiser of their own Order.

"But on these secret principles of theirs, as on Werner's manner of conceiving them, we are only enabled to guess: for Werner, too, has an esoteric doctrine which he does not promulgate, except in dark Sibylline enigmas, to the uninitiated."—*Life and Writings of Werner.*—TRANS.

SCENE III.

Interior of the great Chapel of St. John. Midway in the background, the altar, with life-sized statue of John, and fully illuminated with tapers. In a semi-circle on either side of the altar, covering half the stage, the choir, with the stalls of the Brothers. On the right of the altar, raised by a step, the throne of the MASTER; *to the left opposite him two tabourets, all splendidly decorated. High mass is being celebrated. The* PRESBYTER *of the Order and two* CHAPLAINS *stand before the altar vested in rich chasubles embroidered with the Cross of the Order. Two Choristers ministering in surplices,* MOLAY *and all the Templar-Knights kneeling; the first in the centre, the rest on each side of him, all forming a semi-circle round the altar, and facing towards it.*

PRIESTS OF THE ORDER.
Descend, God's Spirit, bright and clear,
On this Thy band of servants here;
That this world's spirit we despising,
May steadfast towards Thy truth be rising!
Lead us Thyself by Thine own hand,
Into Thy blessed Promised Land,
That we with hearts devout and lowly,
May build Thee there a Temple holy!
                Hallelujah! Hallelujah!
            [He leaves the altar, followed by the two
            CHAPLAINS and preceded by the CHO-
            RISTERS ringing their bells, and around.

MOLAY (who with the other Brothers rises, and takes his seat
            on his chair).
Belovèd Knights and Brothers, take your seats;
I shall, God helping me, a Chapter hold.
            [The KNIGHTS take their places in the Choir,
            the elder on MOLAY'S side of the
            altar, the younger on the other side.
Are all our company assembled here?
Is no one not a Templar in our midst?

            COMMANDER HUGO (standing up).
All are assembled, Valorous Lord and Master,
And there is no intruder on the Chapter.

            MOLAY.
Then in the name of Father, Son and Spirit,
And of Our Lady, I open now the Chapter.
Stand up, belovèd brethren, and pray God
To pour down over us His heavenly grace.
            [Pause, during which all the Brothers stand
            up, in front of their seats, and pray
            with covered faces, and then resume
            their places, sitting down.
Belovèd Knights and Brothers! Many of you
Are willing two new brethren to receive;
Peers, both, of highest birth, Frank of Poitou,

And Adalbert, the Count of Anjou-Maine.
Doth any one of you know ought whereby
They may not lawfully and meetly be
Received as brethren here, let him speak out;
For better were it we should hear it now,
Than later, when they in our presence stand. (*Pause.*)
Does no one speak? They are elected then!
Therefore, go both, you Brother Seneschal,
And Brother Marshal,
     [COMMANDER HUGO *and the* MARSHAL *rise
      from their seats.*
   to the elected twain,
And notify to them, as stands prescribed,
The austerity and compassion of the Order;[1]
And if they will endure it for God's sake,
And give you speech and answer meet to all
Ye shall in virtue of your office ask,
Then you shall come back to us and repeat
All that you've heard from them as told to you.
    [*Exeunt the* COMMANDER *and the* MARSHAL.
  (*To* CHARLOT, *who stands by the door.*)
Go fetch me hither Brother Cyprianus.
         [*Exit* CHARLOT.
   (*To the Assembly.*)
Belovèd Knights and Brothers! Ye are aware
In what terms yesterday his Holiness
Enjoined me, by an autographic brief,
With sixty others of the Temple Order,
For Poictiers to take ship without delay,
There to deliberate of a new Crusade.

  (CHAPLAIN CYPRIANUS *and* CHARLOT *come in; the latter
    resumes his place by the door.*)

  MOLAY (*to the* CHAPLAIN, *to whom he gives a paper*).
Read out the letter, Brother Cyprianus.

[1] Rule LVIII. "If any Knight out of the mass of perdition, or any secular man, wishes to renounce the world, and to choose your life and community, he shall not be immediately received, but, according to the saying of Paul, *Prove the spirits whether they be of God:* and if so, let him be admitted. Let the rule, therefore, be read in his presence," &c. —*Trans.*

CHAPLAIN (*reads*).
"We, Clement, Bishop, Servant of God's servants,
Present to thee, beloved son, and Master
Of the Temple Order of Jerusalem,
James Bernard Molay, greeting from ourselves,
And blessing apostolic primarily!—
Whereas the Lord commands us to effect
And carry on the weal of Christendom
So far as we his worthless servants may;
And it would almost seem the Church of God
Might in these latter and degenerate times
Be swallowed up by impious Antichrist;
We therefore have resolved, inspired by God,
And in all humbleness and holy fear,
Once more to take up arms in faith, and send
The Cross unto Jerusalem, to snatch
The city from the heathen's guardianship;
Further, the Most Christian, and Catholic,
Our well-loved sons, with him of England too,
Themselves, and aided by their vassalage
And Saxons, have determined to take up
Christ's holy Cross; wherefore, right fatherly,
We summon thee to us, dear son de Molay,
And charge thee to repair with sixty more
Knight-Brothers of the Temple to Poictiers,
With utmost haste and minimum of delay,
And there present thyself before our Chair;
Because, thy wisdom being well known to us,
We would take counsel with thee, seeing thou
Thyself hast borne the banner of the Lord
With fame and glory in the Holy Land,
And knowest well all the roads and streams and ports.
We hope, thou wilt, as fits a pious son,
Conform thyself to our paternal will.
Likewise, the Master of the Hospital [1]
We've summoned hither: and we guarantee
Safe conduct to thee, and we will not fail
To hold thee in remembrance in our prayers.

---

[1] As is well known, the Knights of St. John were called Knights of the Hospital of St. John at Jerusalem.

Given at Poictiers in the Datary,
Year of our Lord, thirteen hundred and six,
And the third year of our Apostolate.
Vincent Albano, Cardinal Promotor."
　　　　　　　　[*Gives the paper back to the* MASTER.

　　　　　　　　CHARLOT.
The Elders have returned.

　　　　　　　　MOLAY.
　　　　　　　　　　Let them come in!
　　　(*To the* CHAPLAIN.)
And, Chaplain, you will for a space retire.
　　　　　　　　　　　　[*Exit* CHAPLAIN.

　COMMANDER HUGO *and* MARSHAL *of the Order approach.*

　　　　　　　　MOLAY.
Have you made trial of the Acolytes?

　　　　　　　　COMMANDER.
My Lord and Master, as in duty bound,
We have held converse with the Knights who wait
Without, and clearly have disclosed to them
Our Order's rigour, as we have proved and known;
But they maintain their first desire, to be
Our Order's slaves and soldiers. Answer meet,
And all due speech, they gave the questions asked
By us, as it behoved us; therefore, now,
From this time forward, nothing hinders them
From greeting us as Brethren, if so be
God's pleasure, yours, and all the Brotherhood's.

　　　　　　　MOLAY (*to the Assembly*).
If there be any here, belovèd Knights
And Brothers, knowing any cause whereby
These may not rightly join us here as brethren,
Let him speak out, for better now than later.
　　　　　　　　(*Pause.*)
'Tis then your will that we admit them both,
In God's name, to our confraternity?

All the KNIGHTS.
Yes, let them, in the name of God, come in!

MOLAY (*to the two old Men*).
Go out, then, to them, ancient Knights and Brothers,
And ask them if their resolution holds;
And if they answer, Yes, instruct them how
'To plead for their admission in right terms.'
                    [*Exeunt* COMMANDER *and* MARSHAL.
            (*To the Assembly.*)
Your ears just now have heard the Brief read out,
Sent to us by the Holy Father. Clear
Its meaning is, and leaves no room for doubt;
Yet since the Order, from its earliest rise,
Maintains its rights to scrutinize and choose,
And we, although we honour Peter's chair,
Yet are not, like priests bound by cloister rule,
Thereunto subject with obedience blind;
But are, much rather, knights of noble birth,
Not vassals and not serfs to any man,
But free, with power to do and leave undone,
And prove intelligently which course is best:
We therefore, in the strength of this our right,
I and the Elders, held prolonged debate
Whether the call with free-will to obey,
Or else remain where now we are, at home;
For weighty is the step, and counsel sage
Dissuades crude rashness with too late regret.
But now we have, after long earnest search,
Decided that it best becomes the free
To show to all men an intrepid front;
And even if, beside the said Crusade
Of which there is clear mention in the Brief,
The Holy Father mean yet something more
Than he has written (as is their custom there),—
We yet, undaunted, calling on our God,
And trusting boldly in our righteous cause,

---

¹ Rule LVIII. If it please the Master and the brothers to receive him, let the brothers be called together, and let him make known with security of mind his desire and petition unto all.— *Trans.*

To-morrow will take ship bound for Poictiers,
Whereby we shall—Fate favouring our intent,—
Securely reach the Templar-House at Paris,
And bring a greeting to my brother Philip.[1]

CHARLOT.
The good men with the Acolytes are here.

MOLAY.
Let them come in, and call the Chaplain back.
[*Exit* CHARLOT.

Enter FRANK *and* ADALBERT *dressed as before, who take their position before the Master's chair, facing him. The* COMMANDER *and* MARSHAL *of the Order, who come in behind them, at once take their former places.*

FRANK (*to* MOLAY).
Sir! we are come as suppliants to pray,
Here, before God and you and all the Knights,
For love of God and of our Lady dear,
Your leave to join your confraternity,
And share in all the Order's holy work,
As men who henceforth are resolved to be
The Order's slaves and soldiers all their lives.

MOLAY (*to the Acolytes*).
Dear brothers, 'tis a solemn thing you ask
Who do but see the Order's outer shell:
Ay! but the outer shell!—When ye behold
Our splendid steeds and brilliant equipage,
See that we eat well, drink well, well are clad,
Ye dream, that ye shall profit being with us,
Yet know not how severe the inner rule;
'Twere hard for you, being your own masters now,
To make yourselves the slaves of other wills;
For scarcely shall ye licence find to do
Or leave undone, those things yourselves would wish.
Would you remain on land this side the sea,
You'll be sent over to the other side;

[1] Meaning King Philip the Fair, whom the Master, having princely rank, styles his brother.

Would you in Cyprus be, you'll oft be sent
To Apulia, Naples, Lombardy, to France,
To England, or to lands of other lords,
Where we still keep Preceptories; would ye sleep,
Ye will be told to watch, and would ye watch,
Ye will be sent to bed; when ye would eat,
Ye'll be sent to the stables. Greatly, too,
'Twould disadvantage both yourselves and us
If ye should harbour anything concealed;
See here (*holding before them an open Gospel*) the holy
    Evangel, word of God,
And answer frankly with unvarnished truth,
All questions that I now shall ask of you,
For if ye answer lies, ye are foresworn
And of our Order quit,—which God forbid!

           ADALBERT.
We speak the truth, as Knights are bound to speak.

           MOLAY.
Then first I ask you, both and separately,
Have you a woman, wedded or betrothed,
Who could lay claim to you by canon-law?

           FRANK.
I ne'er was wed.

           ADALBERT.
        A widower am I,
For my betrothed they hurried to her grave.

           MOLAY.
In any other Order have you served?
In any, have you sworn your oath and vow?

           FRANK.
No Order have I entered.

           ADALBERT.
           Nor have I.

MOLAY.
Owe you to any layman any debt,
Which neither you yourself, nor through a friend,
Without our Order's help can liquidate?

FRANK.
I nothing owe.

ADALBERT (*Aside*).
To one great secularist
I owe yet somewhat; but he shall be paid.

MOLAY.
Are you quite sound in body and in mind?
Have you no secret blemish or disease?

FRANK.
I am quite healthy.

ADALBERT.
I have no disease.

MOLAY.
Have you to no layman or Templar-Knight,
Or any other person, promised gold,
Reception in our Order to secure;
And are you quite pure from all simony?

FRANK.
I would not so disgrace yourselves and me.

ADALBERT.
How should I purchase what may not be bought?

MOLAY.
Are you a Paladin of gentle birth?
In honourable wedlock were you bred?
And sprang your father from a knightly race,
And was your mother a lady nobly born?

FRANK.

Henry, my father is, Lord of Poitou,[1]
Seneschal, and a Peer of France's crown,
My mother's lineage borders on the throne;
Matilda, Countess of Bretagne, is she.

ADALBERT.

My father is poor Philip of Anjou;[2]
My mother—oh! be lenient to these tears!—
Was Anna, Flanders' murdered daughter, alas!

MOLAY.

Is either of you Priest or Chaplain? Have
You holy ordination e'er received?

FRANK.

A literate I, but not a priest.

ADALBERT.
Nor I.

MOLAY.

Have you been ever in the Church's ban?

---

[1] Poitou became English property as part of the appanage of Eleanor, wife of Henry II., but was taken from John by Philip Augustus, whose son and successor Louis VIII. left the province to his son Alfonse. Alfonse dying without heirs, Philip III. re-united Poitou to the crown. The Counts of Brienne were a noble family of France. One of them, previous to Molay's time, was elected King of Jerusalem, and afterwards Emperor of Constantinople; but no Henry of Brienne is recorded amongst the numerous biographies of members of that family. A seneschal is a high official under the crown, answering to Lord High Marshal.—*Trans.*

[2] Anjou and Maine came to the crown of England through Henry II.'s mother, Matilda, who married Geoffrey of Anjou and Maine; but they were taken from John by Philip Augustus. Louis VIII. left them to his son Charles, whose brother Louis IX. obtained from Henry III. of England full renunciation of his claims to them. Charles of Anjou, brother of St. Louis, became King of the two Sicilies, and afterwards of Naples only; and Charles of Valois, brother of Philip IV. (the Fair), obtained from the King of Naples the cession of these provinces, Anjou and Maine. So that there is no place in history for Werner's Philip, Duke of Anjou, Prince of the Blood, and banished by Philip IV.—*Trans.*

FRANK and ADALBERT.
No.

MOLAY (*to the Assembly*).
You have heard them. Speak then, elder Knights!
Remains there anything to ask them?

THE ANCIENT KNIGHTS.
No.

MOLAY (*to the Acolytes*).
Dear brethren, I conjure you both once more,
Beware ye tell us nothing but the truth!

FRANK.
A Knight I am.

ADALBERT.
Am I not Anjou's son?

MOLAY (*to* CHARLOT, *who has come in again during the fore-
goIng scene*).
So be it then! Now let the priests come in!
   [CHARLOT *opens the door to the Acolytes, whilst
         he and all the Knights stand up.*
But ye, mark well what I shall say to you!

[*Two Choir boys, each carrying a cushion
on which lie the insignia of the
Order, namely, the Mantle, the Cross
of red cloth, and the Girdle of white
linen, which they deposit on the two
tabourets standing opposite the seat of
the* GRAND MASTER. *Two* CHAPLAINS
of the Order and the PRESBYTER *of
the Order in mass vestments come in.*

[*The* PRESBYTER *and the two* CHAPLAINS
*go to the Altar, and place themselves
before it, their faces towards the as-
sembly.* MOLAY *passes in front of*

them, going to the right-hand side of the altar; the two Acolytes kneel opposite to him, on the left. The Knights leave their seats and place themselves in a semicircle round the altar.

MOLAY (*to the Acolytes, holding before them the open Gospel*).
Do you to God and our dear Lady vow,
To render true obedience all your lives
Unto the Temple's Master, and Commander?

FRANK and ADALBERT (*laying their forefinger on the book*).
Yes, Sir, God helping.

MOLAY.
Do you to God and our dear Lady vow,
To live in chastity your whole lives long?

FRANK and ADALBERT.
Yes, Sir, God helping.

MOLAY.
Do you to God and our dear Lady vow,
To keep all the praiseworthy usages
And ritual of our Order all your life,
And loyally to share our poverty?

FRANK and ADALBERT.
Yes, Sir, God helping.

MOLAY.
Do you to God and our dear Lady vow,
Your life's devotion in chivalric strife
To wrest the Holy Land from hostile hands,
And to defend it manfully when won?

FRANK and ADALBERT.
Yes, Sir, God helping.

MOLAY.
Lastly—do you to God and our dear Lady vow,

Never to look upon the Order as
Stronger or weaker, worse or better, without
Permission of the Master and Convention?

FRANK.
In the name of God!

ADALBERT.
All this we truly vow!

[*The Choir boys remove from the two ta-
bourets the cushions with the insignia,
and holding them place themselves on
each side of the* MASTER, *facing the
Acolytes.*

MOLAY (*to the Acolytes*).
Then in the name of God and of our Lady,
And also of St. John, the holy Father,
And in the name of all the Temple-Brothers,
To all works of the Order which have been
From first to last achieved, admit I you,
Your fathers and your mothers and all kin,
And what more there may be for whom you wish it;
Ye on your parts shall Christianly admit
Ourselves to all good works and worthy deeds
Which you have undertaken and would do.
Moreover, water and bread we promise you,
And our strict Order's poor habiliments,
With plenitude of labour, trouble, and need.
And thus devote I you, Frank of Poitou,
And Adalbert of Anjou, to be Templars,
And here invest you with our mantle white,
　　　　　[*Invests them both with the mantle.*
And fasten on your breast the Saviour's Cross,
　　　　[*Fastens the Cross of red cloth on the mantle of each.*
And with the holy Girdle four times gird,
　　　　　[*He girds them both round the waist with the
　　　　　　　　girdle of the Order.*

And give you lovingly the brotherly kiss,
    [*Kisses each upon the breast, raising him from
       the ground as he does it.*
That you may to the Brethren give it back.
    [FRANK *and* ADALBERT *go, one on the
    right, the other on the left side of the
    altar, to all the Brothers, and kiss
    them all upon the breast. Meanwhile
    the* PRESBYTER *of the Order and the*
    CHAPLAIN *sing, standing before the
    altar, but without any instrumental
    accompaniment.*

 Oh! how delightful,
 How good and joyful
 'Tis to see Brethren
  In unity dwell!

 Precious as ointment
 From the head dropping,
 From the High-priest's head,
  Down to his skirts;

 Like dews of Hermon
 On Zion's mountains,
 Doth the Lord's blessing
  On unity fall.[1]

    [*The* MASTER *and the* KNIGHTS *resume their
    places. The two Acolytes advance
    in front of the altar, where they kneel
    down facing the Priests.*

  PRESBYTER *of the Order* (*to the Acolytes*).
May the Lord bless you and be your defence;
The Lord redeem and purify your souls,
The Lord with his own strength invigorate you.
And herewith, as my Brothers, kiss I you,
    [*Kissing each on the breast.*
And send you to the Master's feet again.
    [*Exit, with the Chaplains and Choir boys,
    in the same order as before.* FRANK

---

[1] The 133rd Psalm, which is chanted by the Priests according to the ritual of Reception into the Order.

and ADALBERT *approach the seat of the* MASTER *and sit down at his feet, upon a carpet spread beneath his chair.*

MOLAY (*reading out of a book which has been handed to him by a Knight*).
Now sit, and let the words I speak thrill through you;
And if your heart of hearts observe them meetly,
The Temple will its doors throw open to you.
You now are with the Order joined completely,
Which many great things has begun with power,
Broods greater yet within her soul, discreetly.
But not yet breaks the mist in clearing shower;
The red Cross casts its gleam athwart midnight,
But pales before the sun's full noontide hour.
And all you've heard to-day, your souls with might
Subduing, wells from that source, pure and holy,
The parent, in this world, of warm delight.
But not yet grows your darkness clear, for slowly
Wears out the night; only the lightning's blazes
Are brief and swift; therefore not yet ye wholly,
Of all that, heard this day, your soul amazes,
Can penetrate the innermost foundation;
But I'll make plain to you *my* utter'd phrases.
When first before my chair ye took your station,
I asked if you were married yet, you noted:
Here no wife's husband meets with acceptation,
For him God hath to one alone devoted,
While we but seek the Great, Pure, Unaffected
By Recompense; for man's proof-armour-coated
Only by sacrifice. Were you connected
With other league, I asked. Our Cross demandeth
From all its devotees a heart deflected
To unshared union with it. I asked, commandeth
Some layman you as debtor? Subjugated
Is borrower to lender. Here none standeth
Accepted, unless free. Nor, enervated
By sickness, bodily or mental, nears
This altar any man; this instigated
My fourth demand; because 'tis strength that rears

The child Perfection. The sick soul conceiving
Acts not, while effluent from Life's sap appears
Activity. I asked if for achieving
This Order, you'd need gold? That metal base
Chokes and contaminates beyond retrieving
The fount of noble thought. From lofty race,
Not causelessly I asked, are you descended?
High birth's a loan, to spur you and to brace;
You'll lay it off what time your course is ended.
I asked if you had been as Priests ordained?
Each for sweet works of blessing are intended,
Most unlike us: the swordsman's weapon's stained
With slaughter ere he bless. Last,—with good cause—
I asked if you were excommunicate;
The sin-beset contends for Truth's pure laws
With little spirit. Now, when we heard, with great
Joy for yourselves and us, you'd passed unshaken
The ordeal, gladly was my heart elate.
You were found worthy of the vow you've taken,
Which sworn to at the sacred hour, midnight,
Must never be through life till death forsaken.
Ye swore obedience; for the governing might,
The lever's, must command each wheel-spoke's turning.
One executes, though many co-unite
In work. To curb desire with manful spurning,
Ye swore. The Mother-Maid draws near the pure
Alone, but no voluptuary is earning
Admission to the hallowed Land.—Ye swore
Assent to Poverty. For wealth withholden
Makes pilgrim-journeys hard to travel o'er;
The steel must shine well-polished but not golden.
In holy conflict to wax weary never,
Ye swore moreover, like the Masters olden;
That is our Circle's uttermost endeavour.
For only endless war wins endless peace,
And nothing but the sword the Palm can sever:
To win your meed, tax your own energies.
Your last vow was humility and trust,
Your eye, however far ahead it sees,
You must to see but what we show, adjust.
Since you're resolved all this to accomplish truly,

I've given you to share our penury's crust,
And Brothers of the Cross ordained you duly;
While, subject to the Order, you've laid by
Henceforth all action's scope, all thought unruly.
The rights you owned, this day sepultured lie.
Wherefore, to each new member, for his wearing
We hand a hueless robe ere he draw nigh[1]
Whereto the Master's hand, with thoughtful caring,
May one day tint significant supply;
A sacred blood-red sign this robe is bearing,
Because you can through blood and death alone
Attain the Highest. We keep the interpretation
Of the intersected triangle unshown,
And its prime wearer; haply in reservation
For you; but shun lies' brood, and mark this zone,
And what it shows you, which, in midway station,
Your higher from your lower parts divides,
And yet unites them with a fair adorning.
A flame there is that in the ether bides,
And where the higher powers revolve is burning,
And in pure hearts of men; this flame's ray rides
Aloft, and sevenfold cleft, to colour turning,
The azure dyes, the sea, the pastures green,
Cloud-lands to us and aëry forms unsealing.—
When in our breasts these fervent rays convene,
They melt, strange phantasies to sense revealing:
Our germs, expanding all to bloom are seen.—
With such a vision o'er our league soft stealing
The tender Father did its morn endow,
Which turned to flowery plains its desert places.
He only, whom adorns the girdle now
Of innocence, which as a fillet graces
That mystic head, can hope himself that brow
To see one day; if, too, his heart embraces
That holiest joy, high love of humankind,
Whose gage the girdle is. Take it! It guideth

---

[1] Rule XX. To the professed Knights, both in winter and summer we give, if they can be procured, white garments, that those who have cast behind them a dark life may know that they are to commend themselves to their Creator by a pure and white life, &c.—*Trans.*

The Idol in the promised land to find,
Which far off, yet attainable, abideth,
Since One, not God, once found it.'—Kiss; with mind
Thought-filled, go, work, say nought, whatsoe'er betideth.'
                         [*Exeunt* FRANK *and* ADALBERT.

(*To the Assembly, having sat down the book.*)
Before we close, beloved Knights and Brothers,
A painful task is left me to fulfil,
The Brother Robert of Heredon, my charge,
Whom I have cherished with a father's heart,
And who has never, never wrought me grief,—
The Knight Sir Robert of Heredon yesterday
Rudely transgressed against our reverend Brother
The Seneschal, and lately Grand Commander;
He failed to mount guard at the Order's watch;
Without my order, he pursued with six,—
The Order's Horse,—the Turkish privateer,
And though he captured him right valiantly,
Yet grossly thereby he infringed the law.
And when for this the Brother Seneschal
Was reprimanding him, he roughly turned
On him, and gripped him on the breast, and tore
The sacred belt from off his mantle. Speak
Now therefore, Ancient Knights, and rightly judge,

' This mysterious language appears to point, not to the " sweet vision of the Holy Grail," but to some vision of a head, to be seen only by the pure. Molay speaks of it as the Idol, and no mere vision, just as the Holy Grail was no phantom, but the cup itself from which our Lord drank at the Last Supper, and which Sir Galahad was pure enough to meet " face to face," and Sir Percival to " behold afar off."

    "Oh, Galahad, Galahad," said the King, "for such
    As thou art, is the vision, not for these."

The Head had from the earliest times been an object of eastern mystical cultus, and the idea had been imported into Europe by the Crusaders, together with the dragons and winged horses and other dreams of the East. St. George's (supposed) head was kept sacred, in silver, in more than one place. Roger Bacon possessed a head which was supposed to speak. Molay perhaps is thinking of a glorified state of the mummy-head mentioned in the last Act—possibly of John the Baptist, who was worshipped by one Asiatic sect.—*Trans.*

' In several articles of the Rule, the brethren are enjoined to speak sparingly.—*Trans.*

E'en as yourselves ye also would be judged.

     COMMANDER (*rising*).
Accord me leave to speak I pray, dear Lord!

      MOLAY.
'Tis granted you!

     COMMANDER.
    Sir Knights, belovèd Brethren!
The thing is as the Master told it, true,
But yet the offence is not so raven-black;
For any roughness I'm alone to blame,
God mend it!—If my old hot head had not
Struck fire, the good youth never would have dreamt
Of being so choleric with his old friend.
Dear Knights, I am no man of many words,
I am indeed ashamed, God mend it, here
To make confession like a serving-brother
At penance; but the valiant Robert, he
Hath not deserved we should so sternly judge
A first offence; so, this while, let it pass;
Take off his mantle for a fortnight: so
Have done with it.   [*Sits down.*

   A YOUNGER KNIGHT (*standing up*).
    The Seneschal is right!

    ANOTHER (*of the same*).
He is so young!

    A THIRD (*standing up*).
   Our bravest and our best!

    A FOURTH (*of the same*).
Did he not win three horsetails?

     MOLAY.
      Silence, there!
Permission was not given you to speak!—
     [*The Knights sit down.*

(*To the Marshal.*) Marshal! You're free to speak, what saith
    the rule?

                  MARSHAL (*stands up*).
Whoso lays hands on his superior,
Or damages the Order's holy belt,
Hath in the Order neither part nor lot.
Whoever is of three great faults accused
Must in the little cell with loaf of bread
And jug of water, be immured, and yield
His soul unto the Lord; thus saith the rule.'

                  COMMANDER (*starting up*).
God mend it, Marshal!—With your leave, Lord Master!
If ye thrust Robert in the little cell,
Then let my grey head bear him company,
For no such deal will old Hugh overlive!

                 Many KNIGHTS (*standing up*).
Pardon for Robert! For our own good Robert!

' Among the many interesting objects, says Mr. Addison, to be
seen in the ancient church of the Knights Templars, is a penitential cell,
a dreary place of solitary confinement formed within the thick wall of
the building, only four feet six inches long and two feet six inches wide,
so narrow and small that a grown person cannot lie down within it. In
this narrow prison the disobedient brethren of the ancient Templars
were temporarily confined in chains and fetters, in order that their souls
might be saved from the eternal prison of hell! The hinges and catch
of a door firmly attached to a doorway of this dreary chamber, still
remain, and at the bottom of the staircase is a stone recess or cupboard
where bread and water were placed for the prisoner. In this cell Brother
Walter de Bacheler, Knight and Grand Preceptor of Ireland, is said to
have been starved to death for disobedience to his superior, the Master
of the Temple. His body was removed at daybreak and buried by
Brother John de Stoke and Brother Radulph de Barton in the middle of
the court between the church and the hall.

    The Temple discipline in the early times was very severe; disobedient
brethren were scourged by the Master himself in the Temple Church,
and frequently whipped publicly on Fridays in the church. Adam de
Valainecurt, a deserter, was sentenced to eat meat with the dogs for a
whole year, to fast four days in the week, and every Monday to present
himself naked at the high altar to be publicly scourged by the officiating
priest.—*See* CAPELL's *Old London, by Walter Thornbury*, vol. i. p. 152.
—*Trans.*

MOLAY.
Silence before the Master and the Chapter!
The next who doth the holy silence break
Shall this day lose his robe for fourteen days,
And on the ground partake of lenten fare.[1]
        [*The* COMMANDER, MARSHAL *and* KNIGHTS
          sit down.
        (*To the* MARSHAL.)
You are quite right, respected Brother Marshal,
As you have said it, so the law decrees.
Thus have we at our consecration sworn;
And would we Justice unimpaired maintain
We must not swerve from it by one hair's breadth!
There's no more shameless use of tyranny
Than nullifying law for favour's sake:
And law-abiding are free Templar-Brothers;
'Tis only slavery that knows no law.
Nevertheless this case is one wherein—
As rightly urged our reverend Seneschal—
The rule's full rigour should not be enforced.
For Heredon is young, it is his first,
His only fault; his exploits might beseem
No simple stripling, but the first of Knights,
Ay, even the man who carries Hugo's sword.
All this avails—not to exonerate him—
But to the lessening of his punishment.
Doth it content you, ancient Knights and Brothers,
That from the Order I now banish him
For ever, and to the world restore him?

    The Ancient KNIGHTS (*rising from their seats*).
                  Ay!

    MOLAY (*promptly standing up, with raised voice*).
Be it then known, Sir Robert of Heredon,
Knight-Templar, from the Order is dismissed.
From sin and frowardness, Lord, deliver us!
    (*After he and all the Elders have reseated themselves,*
        to CHARLOT.)
Hath he been summoned, as I gave command?

[1] One of the minor punishments of the Order.

CHARLOT.
E'en now he waits without.

MOLAY.
Let him come in. [CHARLOT *goes*.

COMMANDER (*standing up*).
Grant me permission, Master, to retire.
The youth, God mend it! else will break my heart!

MOLAY (*to the* COMMANDER).
Go, Brother Seneschal! (*To* GOTTFRIED.) You, Gottfried, lead
Sir Hugo to his cell.
[*Exit* COMMANDER, GOTTFRIED *leading him*.

ROBERT (*in his shirt and underclothing only, with a rope round his neck, led in by* CHARLOT).

MOLAY (*to* ROBERT).
Draw nearer, Robert!
(*To* CHARLOT.) Take the rope off him.
[CHARLOT *takes the rope from* ROBERT'*s neck, and goes back to the door.*

MOLAY (*Aside*).
Scarce can I restrain
My feelings any longer—God, O God!—
(*To* ROBERT.) Come here to me! The offence charged on
this paper,—
Feel'st thou that thou art guilty of it?—
[*Shows him the paper.*

ROBERT (*after reading it*).
Yes.

MOLAY.
Hast anything to say on thy behalf
Might mitigate thy fault?

ROBERT (*much moved*).
No.

MOLAY.
                    Dost thou know
What punishment, according to our rules,
Now waiteth thee?

                    ROBERT.
                    Death in the little cell.

                    MOLAY.
Gravely thou hast offended, Heredon!
'Tis true thou hast by manly deeds, erewhile,
And by obedience and submission now,
Kept, in integrity, thy vow to us;
Yet even a life-time stainless bateth not
The endless consequences of one crime.
            (*With ever increasing emotion.*)
Thee as our valiant Brother we have loved;
'Twas thy first fault, poor Robert, for which cause,
Our Order mitigates its rule severe;
It gives thee life, and sorrowing gives thee back
Unto that world whence it uprooted thee
To plant thee in its beauteous Paradise.
Go home, my son!—This once the Master may
Melt and be man!—My noble nursling, go!
Be mindful of thy lofty powers and parts;
They beckon thee to duties grave and high—
The Eternal lets no grain of seed-corn fail;
Take my last blessing for a parting gift.
(ROBERT *kneels to him. He lays his hand on* ROBERT's
    head. Tears start from his eyes, and he says softly to
    ROBERT, *who in deepest emotion wipes them away for him*)
So!—Dry my weary eyelids! We shall meet
Hereafter, through the portals of decay!
(*Inspired.*) Ah! 'tis an angel's wing sweeps over me!
A phœnix rises from my funeral urn!
            [*Sinks fainting back into the chair.*

                    A KNIGHT.
What ails the Master?

                    ANOTHER.
                    He is pale as death!

A THIRD.

His eyes he closes!

RUSSET (*starting up, overcome with emotion*).
Die, thou noble soul!
[*Rushes out*, CHARLOT *after him*.

MARSHAL (*approaching* MOLAY).
By your leave, most valorous Master, you're not well.

CHARLOT (*brings in a goblet, offering it to the* MASTER).
This cordial swallow!

MOLAY (*after he has drunk*).
I thank thee. It was but
A passing weakness. Is he gone?—

CHARLOT.
E'en now
He went.

MOLAY (*looks up suddenly*).
Is't mere illusion of mine eyes?
Doth it not lighten violently?

A KNIGHT.
Yes,
A fearful storm is gathering in the west.

MOLAY.
Well, we'll be brief.
(*To the Assembly, after* CHARLOT *has returned to his place.*)
Forgive an old man's weakness,
And if't be possible, grant me one request,
Which long I have cherished in my inmost heart.
I go my way to France,—the days of man
Are numbered,—it might easily befall
That I returned no more. Full fain would I
Go to my fathers burdened by no curse!
I hope there's no man living curses me,
Who have done no conscious wrong to any man;

Yet one I know of who in prison groans ;
True, 'twas the Chapter's sentence ; still he groans,
And fain am I to dry all tears, and close,
'Mid cheerful looks, my grand account with fate.
You know Prior Heribert of Montfaucon,
How long in vain he languisheth to meet
The light of day, the sun's enkindling beam !
He's no ignoble man, the Order much
Has been beholden to him—set him free !

PRECEPTOR.
Thy deadly foe ?

An Old KNIGHT.
The infamous heretic ?

MOLAY.
The Eternal judge his faith ! For Enmity,—
'Tis but the severance of two sister souls ;
That, oft, which seems a dark cloud seen from far,
Shines out a noble temple, nearer drawn.
Each man, thank God, to whom the human form
Is his fair heritage, more beauty wins
As we draw nearer him in faith and trust ;
Aye, ev'n although it squint, in every eye
The clear reflection of the skies is seen ;
Grant me then nearer access to the Prior,
Who, did he know me better, might perchance
Forget to see the cast that's in mine eye [1]—
Dear Brethren, grant me freedom for the Prior ! (*Pause.*)
Ye nod assent ? Now then, I thank you for it !
Charlot, at daybreak, go to him, and lead
Him to me, so from mine own lips to learn
He owns the bliss of freedom long desired.
Now call the Presbyter to benediction ! [*Exit* CHARLOT.
    (*Opening the Ritual book of the Order, he reads.*)
" Beloved Knights and Brothers, we may now
Well close the Chapter ; for by God's will, all

---

[1] In the portrait on the title-page of the original, Molay has, really, a decided cast in his eye.—*Trans.*

Goes well, and that the Good be permanent
And ever still increase and grow to more,
May God and our dear Lady grant, I pray."

        [*Enter* CHARLOT *with the* PRESBYTER *of the
Order, in black mass-gown with the red
Cross, holding an hour-glass in his
hand, who stops directly in front of
the* MASTER, *whereupon the latter and
all the Brethren stand up.*

        PRESBYTER.
The sand runs out!—Bethink you of your sins!
        [MOLAY *and all the Brethren kneel down.*

        MOLAY (*kneeling*).
Stand not in judgment with thy servants, Lord!
        [*He and all the Knights kiss the ground: the*
        PRESBYTER *blesses them. Solemn pause.*

        MOLAY
(*Stands up and stretches his arms towards the Assembly*).
You by my power as Master I absolve;
        [*After all the Brethren have risen to their feet.*
Ye likewise will discharge me of my debt!

        The Ancient KNIGHTS.
The mercy we receive we yield again.

        MOLAY (*taking the* PRESBYTER *by the hand.*)
Come, Presbyter, say, after ancient use,
The song of peace with me, that so the Lord
May look with favour on the Templar League!
        [*He goes with him to the Altar, where both,
hand in hand, face the Assembly. In
exactly the same position, but facing
the altar, and with bowed heads and
backs bent, the Brethren approach
the Altar in pairs one after the other,
so that they form a double row with
the* MASTER *and the* PRESBYTER.

Thy peace, O Lord of might, give unto us!
By peace alone thy works are prosperous.—
That in thy strife we weary not nor cease,
Grant us thy peace!

PRESBYTER.
Give peace, that so Jerusalem the true,
The overthrown, may be rebuilt anew;
And ne'er the Church to this world's spirit may
Become a prey!

MOLAY.
As to our fathers who to thee gave life,
Give peace to us who wander still in strife;
Give hope that he who, striving, fights shall wear
Faith's palm-crown fair!

ₗPRESBYTER.'
So shall in wisdom, beauty, strength divine,
At last, the Temple's seven wonders shine.
O'er faith, and hope and love, our heavenly dower,
Death wields no power.
[*They embrace one another, then the
Knights go slowly away in pairs,
followed at last by* MOLAY *and the*
PRESBYTER.

CHAPLAIN CYPRIANUS (*creeps out from behind the Altar,
where he has been hidden during the preceding scene*).
You and your peace the Devil fly away with!
If he release them, God have mercy on us!—

BELL-RINGER OTTO (*anxiously opens the door and peeps in*).
Sir!

CHAPLAIN (*low*).
Otto!

OTTO (*coming in*).
Oh! I'm as wet as if I'd swum!

CHAPLAIN.
Tell me, for God's sake, Otto! are they off?—

OTTO.
Yes, Sir! by this time in the forest, please God.
Such a to-do we had, Sir!—Montfaucon
Refused to stir. And had the other one,
The red-bearded, not twanged on his guitar
A foolish song, there they'd have been till now.
When his ears caught the tune, the Devil possessed
His legs. And like one sense-bereft and blind
He ran as though sev'n spirits were after him,
Nor stopped for lightning or the lashing hail.

CHAPLAIN.
Another time! Here we might be o'erheard!
'Tis well they're gone. High time indeed, or else
The morn had seen a reconcilement feast,
From which may God deliver us by his mercy!

OTTO.
And now, your Reverence!—Our agreement stands?
The holy father would not tell a lie?—
I'm really Banner-Bearer?

CHAPLAIN.
    Yes, oh yes!
(*Offering him his flask, which he draws from under his robe.*)
Take this small flask for your refreshment—take it,
And now (*pushing him out*) be off, that no one find us here!
    [OTTO *goes away with the flask.*

CHAPLAIN (*alone, looking after him with a sneer*).
In Heaven, thou fool! If my flask please thy palate,
Thy chattering mouth shall gape no more to-morrow!
But hold—Sir Cyprianus, is this sin?—
Nay! Father Vincent says himself: "So long
As there's no scandal, all's permissible."
How better could I scandal obviate than

By giving his *quietus*, pleasantly,—
And following an old custom of the Church,—
To this man whom I've made my tool? Once done,
Then whether it were right or wrong can be
Discussed in the confessional. 'Tis enough,
It leads towards the Pallium!—For the sin,
I shove that under Father Vincent's cowl. [*Exit.*

SCENE IV.

A wild part of the forest, not far from the harbour. Thunder, lightning, and rain. It is now deep midnight. Ex-Prior HERIBERT *rushes in with bare head, and hair on end.* NOFFO, *rather slower, and as if wearied out, behind him. Both in monk's apparel.*

PRIOR (*throwing himself down on a rock*).
Here will I rest me.

NOFFO.
Heribert, what the devil!
You run as if pursued by the wild huntsman!

PRIOR (*listening wildly*).
Hark! Hear'st thou nought?—

NOFFO.
What the fiend should I hear?
The storm so rages one can neither see
One's hand, nor hear the words one's own lips speak!
Yet, am I right, amidst this wild uproar
A sound comes of the roaring of the waves.
Come, haste!—The sea is surely close at hand;
And here 'tis horrible!

PRIOR.
                No, we'll remain!
This wild place pleases me, and beautiful
The night is, as with howls it echoes back
The frenzy raging in me!

                NOFFO (shuddering).
                        Why, it is
A murderous night, as though all fiends were loosed!
Like red-hot witches'-brooms whiz slantingly
The ruddy lightnings—rain pours down in streams,
Mixed with a thousand heavy hail-stones. Fast
And furious fares the unfettered blustering wind
Through all the boughs; all round in the dark forest
Are shrieks and groans, as though old Night brought forth,
In dismal emulation of the storm
Cry owl and jackal!—brr!—'Tis fearful, fearful!

        PRIOR (*starting and drawing* Noffo *to him*).
Hist! Noffo!—look!—See'st not yon little flame?
It has a human aspect.
        (*Springing up and shrinking in terror to one side.*)
                        Noffo, see!
Is it not Molay, whom we would sacrifice?—

                EUDO's VOICE.
Heribert, turn from thine infamy;
Child of the light, let the fire be;
In the Now dwells thine Eternity!

        PRIOR (*breaking into wild laughter*).
Ha! Ha! the thunder speaks! (*suddenly pausing.*)
                Shall I——or?

        NOFFO.
                        Come!—
An 'twere the devil himself—revenge to find!

        PRIOR (*seizing him furiously by the hand*).
Ha!—thank thee, Owlet, for thy lullaby!
Yes, Hell!—Here take my whole self's dedication!—
That laughter, is't the expression of thy joy?

(*To* Noffo.) Come!—for the moment quickly passeth by!
Come!—for our victim's hour is nigh—
Come, mate! we'll share the wages, thou and I!
        [*He rushes out like a madman, dragging
          Noffo along with him.*

       Eudo (*appearing with a lute*).
The night-storm drives him on,
His help's in the Cross alone;—
I wander till to Templars the Temple shall be shown.
Then rest me in the chamber, there with my bride made
    one,
Who seals my union
With HIM by power and love for ever known;
Unending, still beginning, I revel, godlike, on
In the Shall Be, and the Has Been that is gone,
And embrace them with the Present all in one!
        [Eudo *passes on as he utters this rhapsody,
        holding his lute under his arm.*

SCENE V.

MOLAY'S *sleeping cell. The moonlight streams in through an
    open window. It is still night.*

      MOLAY (*sitting alone by the window*).
A fearful hurricane!—So old I am,
Yet ne'er saw such a tempest!—Now praise God!
'Tis over, and the Eternal's levin-flash
Hath only served to purify the air
And our poor dwellings graciously hath spared.
Do like results await us? Will the storm,
That o'er our heads is gathering fearfully,
Our work so purify, and not destroy?
Destroy?—What chaos!—Yet canst thou, mere dust,
Command the flame to purify, whose work

Perhaps, O God! is to annihilate?
My sacristy!—Ye golden halls, that shine
Brilliant as glitter in the night the stars,—
Must ye fall shattered 'mid the Temple's flames?
My thorny crown with which I hoped to bind
These brows that happy myrtle never pressed,
Was't but a dream, a puerile tragedy?—
And must my latest garland also fade?
    (*Tears streaming down his face.*)
Thou Light Eternal, parent thou of flowers!
Is such indeed Thy will?—so must it be?—
(*Pause, during which he gazes, lost in thought, from the
   window down on the still whereore valley.*)
Night shrouds the mirror-surface of the sea;
The moon is hidden in the storm-clouds yet!
  (*Pause, during which light appears in the valley.*)
The cloud is gone, the moon is bright once more,
And like a bridegroom[1] decks the sea with pearls
And smiles,—e'en while he sprinkles tears, he smiles!
And our small ship made ready to depart
Swells out her gleaming sails! The All-Merciful
Bring all to pass according to His will!
(*Pause, during which he looks down cheerfully on the valley
    bathed in moonlight.*)
What sounds of lute (*motioning outside the window*) are those
 I hear without?
So melting soft, as though too kind to wake
The midnight out of her last sleep?—The lute
Draws nearer from the valley upwards. What!
Doth haply some poor luckless Troubadour,
Astray, and wandering from his road, wet through
With rain, and tempest-wearied, seek with us
A hospitable shelter? How!—Deceive
Me not mine ears?—Already in the cloister?
Why, truly this is strange! The lute is playing
At hide and seek! (*Calling.*) Greger!—What! at my door?
Already art thou here? Aërial
Ambassador, come in, whoe'er thou be!
      [*He starts from his seat.*

---

[1] In German, in defiance of mythology, the moon is masculine and the sun feminine.—*Trans.*

Enter EUDO (*dressed as a pilgrim; his face so shrouded that only his beard appears. He carries in his hand his lute, on which he strikes a few notes before speaking*).
Your pardon, Sir, that thus so late I come
With twang of lute!—My wont is on the strings
To herald my approach, and eke the chords
To touch when forth I wander on my way.
     [*Short pause, during which* MOLAY *observes
     him with close attention.*
Permit me to sit down, for I have gone
Far in my pilgrimage of ninety years (*sits down*).

    MOLAY.
Right willingly! But say, how did you gain
Admission here so late?

    EUDO.
     I played without,
First, yonder on the wall. A friendly porter
There opened me the door, and quietly
I glided through and on.

    MOLAY.
     You glided fast,
I' faith!—A moment hence you had just reached
The Cross-vault, and already are you here!

    EUDO.
That is my manner!

    MOLAY.
    Did no one of my guard
Arrest your steps?

    EUDO.
    No—men are never wont
To stop me on my way.

    MOLAY (*with increasing astonishment*).
    Who are you, then?

    EUDO.
A poor bard, I, who in the holy wars
Fought, as men fight, and now, in his old age,

Sings joyously the song of manly jousts
In which he once took part

     MOLAY.
       But what would you
Do here?

     EUDO.
    I'd sing to you one pious song,
And then fare further on my way.

     MOLAY.
       'Tis now
Deep night! Abide until the morrow and court
Repose!—I call my servants!

     EUDO.
       Let them rest!
Blessed are they who from their labours rest!
But stay not me!—For I must further roam
When I have sung my song.

     MOLAY.
       Then sing it me,
Night-raven! but the muffling hood take off
Which masks you from me.

     EUDO.
       I prefer it so!
And now ye antique lute-strings, sound the times
That have been, and the days that are to come!
  (*Sings, accompanying the song with his lute.*)

    When the knell of death tolls down,
    When the martyr wins his crown,
    Then is smoothed the Judge's frown.

    What though hell oppose in ire!
    Polycarp lived on the pyre,[1]
    While his ashes fed the fire.

[1] Polycarp was bishop of Smyrna, and one of the first Christian martyrs. He was burnt because he would not deny his faith; and the legend (legend means "that which may be read") says that in this fiery death he suffered little or nothing.

Death o'er him won no control,
Cool while flames around him roll,
On Jesu was stay'd his soul.

When the ashes had burnt low
He was quit of earthly woe,
Caught up heavenly joy to know.—
Thou, like Polycarp, also!

MOLAY.
A pretty song! Praise to the noble wrestler
For whom Christ wove the holy martyr-crown!

EUDO (*with altered and elevated voice*).
Praise, my brave Molay, be to thee!

MOLAY.
            Whose voice?—
Pray thee unmask thyself!—

EUDO (*in his previous quiet tone*).
            I like it so.

MOLAY.
You spoke to me just now in tones that thrill'd
Through all my nerves!—

EUDO.
            May be! for, after singing,
There lingers sometimes in mine aged throat
A ring of melody.

MOLAY (*Aside*).
            I cannot err;
Yet I must have conviction! (*To the old man.*) Will you not
Be strengthened ere you go with meat and drink?

EUDO.
My part is to feed others, not myself!—

MOLAY.
But wherefrom come you, then, enigmatist?
Where dwell you?

EUDO.
          In the Grey-Friars' monastery
At Acre, the good monks assigned to me
A small rest-chamber. Yet oftwhiles I'm driven
Forth like a sweeping tempest, and, like fate,
I restless roam o'er field and heath and sea,
And enter where good people dwell, by night,
To sing what has been done, and what shall be.

          MOLAY.
At Acre, in the Grey-Friars' monastery!
How strange!—Some forty years ago fell there
My worthy friend and uncle in the fray,
Guarding the Cross's banner; they interred
Him in that very cloister—

          EUDO (*with changed raised voice*).
                    Marshal Eudo?

          MOLAY (*eagerly*).
For Christ's dear wounds' sake! Let me now behold
Thy face, for 'tis mine uncle's voice I hear.
          [*As he presses towards him, EUDO stands
          up, and throws back his blue robe so
          that his golden armour bearing the
          Cross, and the bridal wreath on his
          head are seen.*

          EUDO (*in deeply earnest and solemn tones*).
When torments hedge thee round,
They spring from starry courts that shine before thee,
Let this thought reassure thee;
Love beckons thee through pain!—Be lord of fate,
When flames are curling o'er thee!
Thou art the power that can the stars create!
Fire wastes the Cross, for thee the eternal harps resound.
  (*Cheering himself anew, and reassuming his former tone.*)
Sound, lute-strings, sound, in the cold house of death!
Home to warm cell the old man hasteneth!
          [*Exit, playing on his lute.*
                    P

MOLAY (*hastening after him and calling him*).
Ah, stay yet! Stop him!
(*Hurries after him, and presently comes back, confounded.*)
      'Tis as though the earth
Had swallowed him! Could it be possible?
Or might the sentries———? (*Calling through the door.*)
      Greger! Guido! Hath
The sleep of death turned you to stone?
(GREGER *and two other* MEN-AT-ARMS, *running in hastily.*)

     GREGER.
          Here, Master!

     MOLAY.
Where hold you watch?

     GREGER.
      I watch the cloister, Sir!

    SECOND MAN-AT-ARMS.
And I the door!

    THIRD MAN-AT-ARMS.
    And I the ante-chamber.

     MOLAY.
Saw ye, then, not that pilgrim cloaked in blue,
Carrying a lute, who went from me just now?

    SECOND MAN-AT-ARMS.
We have seen nothing.

     MOLAY.
     Have ye, then, not heard
The music of a lute?

    THIRD MAN-AT-ARMS.
    Nought have we heard.

     MOLAY.
Were ye awake, then?

GERTER.
       Wake enough to hear
The cricket chirping.

       MOLAY.
            It is very strange!
       (*Then to the two* MEN-AT-ARMS)
Go to your posts.   [*They go*.
(*To* GERTER.) But thou make haste to seek
The old man who went forth from me but now;
He must be at the door, or hiding in
The Cloister. Go! Run quickly. Thy reward
Is my dear Tartar if thou find him. Haste!

       GERTER.
At once, Sir!   [*Hastens away*.

       MOLAY.
       Fain I'd sleep—yet slumber flees
Before my spirit's eyes, and many thoughts
Are whirling in wild eddies round my head!
I, dust, that power which can the stars create?
That fire the Cross consuming, and the harps!—
Perhaps illusion.—End all with thy Grace,
O Father! in whose hands myself I place.

ACT VI.

SCENE I.

Temple Garden. In the foreground, PHILIP'S *cottage; in the background, the sea. The morning begins to dawn.*

PHILIP.

NOW morning dawns, out yonder. True, the sun
Yet resteth in the sea: but yon thick clouds,
Exhaling o'er the billows, harbinger
His advent. Why must his approach to us
Be still mist-hidden? When shall we attain
The privilege to see him as he is,
In unveil'd splendour?—Patience still, and hope!
                    [*Going to the flower-beds.*
How the terrific storm of yester-night
Hath comforted my little darlings here,
The flowers!—Night-Violet, hast thou felt no fear?
Poor thing, fear nought!—the devastating flash
Of lightning only strikes the cedar tall;
Small things like you, your very littleness
Protects, and that same hurricane which rends
Rock-masses, to the corn-fields adds new strength.
(*Pause.*) Securely I have slumbered in your midst,
But now once more my fitful destiny
Impels me to the heights. I go, dear friends!
Soon as the warm sun, whose mild friendly beams
Hath fostered you, shall this day from your cheek
Kiss off the tears of joy ye shed to feel
The renovation of your vital powers;
Soon as ye unfold in gladness, to drink in
His ray, your friend will toss on far-off waves

That bear him onwards to return no more,
Ah, certainly no more! (*Pause*.) Farewell, then! Thanks
For every hour of calm delight, for all
Your soothing, all sweet balms exhaled on me,
That which in vain I sought 'mong human kind,—
Proud souls who vaunt themselves creation's kings,—
I've found among you here, in union fair,
Simplicity, love, peace. Ah, never hang,
Lily, thy little head! O God! I might
Be proud indeed had I thy purity!
Thou regal rose!—Not regal, nay, not stained
With blood, like Philip Augustus' robe is thine.¹
Avaunt, detested image! Desecrate
Not thou these homes of calm beatitude!
'Tis past! The stern reality dispels
My fair dream-vision, it has fleetly fled.
Brief are the moments which a man may snatch
From earthly trammels, and into ether soar
On golden pinions; always to be thrust
Down to the inevitable dust again,
And forced into the yoke!—Who cometh here?

  ADALBERT *approaches, completely equipped as Templar.*

     PHILIP.
Ha, Adalbert, is't thou, mine only son?
Hath the past night of terror robbed thee too
Of power to sleep?
     ADALBERT.
    It hath tormented sore
My bleeding heart by stirring up the source
Of torturing memory. In such a night,
O Father, I was widowed. Let me hide
These tear-distilling eyes on your kind breast!

   PHILIP (*taking him in his arms*).
Give thy tears vent. These witnesses of poor
Humanity dishonour not the Knight.

¹ Philip II., called Augustus, was great-great-grandfather of Philip IV., styled the Fair, and went to the Crusade with Richard Cœur de Lion. As Adalbert makes use of the title "Augustus" further on, when speaking of the reigning King, Philip the Fair, Werner must have confused the *sobriquets* of these two kings.— *Trans.*

Oh, break this weary silence which doth vex
Thy father's darkened soul; one day and more
Have we lived through since fate united us!
And still thou hidest, unrevealed to me,
The story of thy woes.

      ADALBERT.
     Oh, Father mine!

      PHILIP.
Am I not that? Oh, think! brief moments now
Remain to us, the vessel claims us soon,
But here we are unwitnessed; Adalbert!
Shall then thy father, shall thine earliest friend,
Shall he who by like sorrow hath been made
Associate in woe, not share thy grief?

  ADALBERT (*who during this speech has been staring
     before him, lost in thought*).
In such a hideous night—yes, I will tell
You all;—though I have long forborne to kill
Your peace with such a poison-breath; enough
That you desire it, and I will!—In such
A night my Agnes gave me her last kiss;
The morrow should our endless union seal:
The guests were ready, everything prepared,
I went from her that evening, light of heart;
The fury of the terrible north-wind
To me seemed airs from Eden. What love is
Tell me yourself, my father!—In its eyes
What shows so black but with a roseate hue
It can invest it?

     PHILIP (*darkly*).
    Truly? Can it that?
Then it shall tint black murder's raven-clouds
For me with blood of ravished roses! (*Excitedly*.) King
Philip!

    ADALBERT (*with enthusiasm*).
   My Agnes' spirit, wilt thou that?—
What, silent still!—

PHILIP.
She will, by Saint Sebastian!
Proceed!

ADALBERT (*collecting himself with difficulty*).
From Agnes' threshold through the streets
I made my rapid way, and with me went
Our servant Humbert. All seemed animate
With joy because the morrow morn should see
Me claim her for my own, my fairest love!
But suddenly, just at the corner, where
The Street Faydeau bends round towards the Seine,
A voice aroused me from my ecstasy:
Ere I could think, a heavy blow behind
Had struck my head and felled me to the earth,
All senseless. When bewildered I awoke,
Lo, I was in a ward of many beds,
Surrounded by the dying and the dead.
A pious maid of that devoted band,
The Sisterhood of Charity, stood, veiled,
By me. I see her still! Right glad was she,
She said, to see my eyes re-open, I
Was numbered with the dead, and had received
Already the last unction, and my knell
Was to be tolled. 'Twas in St. Roch I lay,
The Hospital; and seven days before
A man not known had brought me. I had lain
Unconscious ever since. In vain I sought
To question of her further. With all care
She tended me; but never could I win
Free speech of her; in consolation rich,
And benefits, she had too much to do
For me, and all the rest, than to exchange
Mere words with individuals. When, at length,
Seven suffering weeks lived through, I left my bed
Once more, and turned me from that house, with thanks
To my kind nurse,—(Her constant aim it was
To seem to all poor death-sick folks nought less
Than Agnes to my life is. Daily dying
Herself, in death she lived, like me, but far
More nobly—for she left herself no time

For her own tears, for her own comforting !
God be her comforter, good mistress !)

     PHILIP.
       Then ?

   ADALBERT (*recollecting himself*).
Yes !—When I left St. Roch's hospital
I found our Humbert waiting at the door,
And then the enigma terribly was solved !

   PHILIP (*with ever-increasing curiosity*).
Now !—

     ADALBERT.
Nogaret's[1] paid assassins dealt the blow
That laid me low !

     PHILIP.
   Oh, my presentiment !

     ADALBERT.
Not satisfied with working thine undoing,
Nor with my mother's death, the villain thought
To extirpate the last of the Anjous,
The sole remaining scion of that great tree.
The King's lust smoothed for him the way thereto
For Philip Augustus, the crowned profligate,
Had long cast eyes of covetous desire
On her, my bride, of angel-purity ;
But I stood in his way. Nor wist he how
To reach me with the sharp sword of the law,
Though well the crafty Chancellor Nogaret
Was skilled to wield it. So, to gain this end,
A murderous pack must needs be slipped on me
To slay me on the threshold of my bliss,
And for the royal villain smooth a way
To my beloved Agnes, by my death.
He could not compass it. His deadliest foe

---

[1] Chancellor, and principal minister of Philip IV.—*Trans.*

Still lives, but ah! a lovelier victim fell
The mischiever's prey!

PHILIP.
           And how then didst thou learn
This ghastly news?

ADALBERT.
           My servant, who as soon
As fled the assassins (who all deemed me dead)
Dragged me, that same night, to the hospital,
Swore to the truth of all I tell you now;
For one, a servant of the King and comrade
In arms of Humbert, told him privately,
To warn him of the danger.

PHILIP.
           And thine Agnes?

ADALBERT.
Swiftly the dreadful tidings of my death
Had spread abroad through Paris.

PHILIP.
                    Yes!—thereby
I also was deceived, and my last lock
Of brown hair changed to grey.

ADALBERT.
                    Our Humbert dared
Not gainsay the report, my life at stake,
Scarce dared creep in by stealth at night where I
In hospice lay, nigh locked in death's embrace.
A fortnight had passed by, ere,—oh, too late!—
Had he gone earlier she would have been saved!—
He stole to Agnes' dwelling. There he learnt—
Oh, God Eternal!—Bid me say no more;
These old wounds bleed with two-fold agony!

PHILIP.
They shall not staunch!—Recall the awful oath

Sworn at midnight, at vengeance' sacred shrine,
Think of thy mother, and that final cry
She sent up, in her last birth-giving pangs,
Unto the avenger!

ADALBERT.
                   Oh! a thousandfold
May it fall back again on Philip's head!

                    PHILIP.
Go on!

                    ADALBERT.
          I will!—where was I? Yes!—not till
A fortnight had elapsed did Humbert seek
The house where Agnes dwelt, to learn there how
When tidings reached her of my death she swooned,
A burning fever ravaged her. Her friend
The pious Abbess of St. Clare then caused
Her, in her bed-clothes swathed, to be conveyed
Into the Convent of St. Clare, where, given
The holy Sacrament, she breathed her last
A few days after. To the Convent straight
I sped, and heard the portress there confirm
The truth of Humbert's tale. Then, then would I
Have slaked for ever in the tyrant's blood
My thirst of vengeance, but to Bordeaux he
Was gone, to sell the priest[1] the papal crown,
And watchful were his murder-mongers. Needs
Must I my life preserve to compass his.
And first I wished to make my peace with God
And in the Holy Land seek new-born strength
From Him, for my revenge; so at Marseilles
Embarked, from thence to sail to Palestine;
How then the pirate captured us, to fall
Himself a prey to Heredon, you know!

                    PHILIP.
Enough, enough I know; yet let me ask

[1] Bertrand de Got, Archbishop of Bordeaux,—afterwards Clement V.
— *Trans.*

One question more, my Adalbert! Why thus
Hast thou from me and Molay, with design,
Concealed the station and the parentage
Of thy dear lost one?

ADALBERT.
Father! oh, because—
But why conceal it from you?—Until now
Mere weakness closed my lips, lest I should cast
A slur upon the ashes of my love.
She was what people call the bastard child
Of a high lord—so said report—the fruit
Of intercourse unlawful.

PHILIP.
What then was
Her father's name?

ADALBERT.
I never learnt from her
What name he bore; but she herself was called
Agnes of Clairmont—

PHILIP.
Clairmont? Was her home
Not in the Faubourg Marceau?

ADALBERT.
There she dwelt,
And with her lived her aunt, named Percival.
(*Astonished.*) But what ails you, my Father?

PHILIP (*Aside*).
Terribly
The light dawns on me. (*Aloud.*) Thou didst name but now
The Abbess of St. Clare. Hast never seen her?

ADALBERT.
Once only can I call to mind I saw her,
'Twas when a novice took the veil; a being
Majestical and lofty she did seem.
Soft dignity appeared to me to shine

In her expressive serious countenance
And something else, not just anticipation,
But rather a deep-rooted certainty;
And therewithal such rigid smiling gaze,
As Mary might have worn had she been, by
The angel's greeting, turned to stone, and yet
Full conscious of the Saviour that she bore!
So looked she!

PHILIP (*Aside*).
Molay's sister he beheld!
(*Aloud.*) Tell me, had not thy love a red brown spot
No bigger than a fly near her left eye?—
Just on the temple at that juncture where
The little rivulets of blue veins meet?
Was she not very fair, slender, well-grown,
And—lived she—would she not be now seventeen?

ADALBERT (*with loving enthusiasm*).
Ah! Lived she, so should I live, now and ever!
(*Restraining himself.*)
Yes, Father: thus, O God! her shade I saw,
Yet clothed in form more infinitely fair!
Aye, infinitely! For when my gaze and hers
Then, each with each, were blended, I was not
On earth, nor even in heaven, but in the sea.
My Being interfused with it, streamed out
Through ocean and through earth, through Heaven and Hell,
How she was formed, or were she truly ought,
I knew not, only I was—infinite!

PHILIP.
Come to thyself —(*seizing him by the hand, and observing
      a ring on it*). What is this ring?

ADALBERT (*agitated*).
                                             The ring
Of my betrothal.

PHILIP (*casts another glance at the ring, then hiding his face
      convulsively in both his hands, Aside*).
Molay's!

ADALBERT (*more fully embracing him*).
                                        Ah, dost thou
Feel with me, comrade of my pain?

                    PHILIP.
                                Ask not—
Thee, to my comfort, will the Master take
With him to France; but not yet may'st thou show
Thyself in Paris—there too easily
Thou might'st be recognized, therefore thou shalt
Go only to the Priory Notre Dame,
The Order's first House on the Frankish coast,
And bide there quietly until I send
Thee further news from Paris—Make thee ready;
We go on board at sunrise; but say nought
To Molay, on thine oath, of all these things
We twain have here discoursed. Go, expedite;
The day already dawns!   [ADALBERT *goes*.
                    Alas, poor father!
And pitiable friend! He nothing knows
As yet; but he will hear of it. This cup,
Too, is reserv'd for him!—O Destiny
Inscrutable, most strange!—The offspring, Molay,
Of thy sole friend must all unwittingly
Destroy, alas! thy fair and only flower,
Thy stolen one! and bared of all thy leaves
There thou dost stand, thou lordly Palm-tree, pride
And foremost ornament of all the grove!
          (*Darkly and smiling bitterly.*)
They call me Illuminate, and they say true,
The name of Fate's envenomed dart I know.
'Tis Hazard!—Shines life's *ignis fatuus?* Lo,
'Tis out!—and deathly mists shroud all the view.   [*Exit.*

SCENE II.

The Master's Hall, as at the commencement of Act III. COMMANDER HUGO, *fully equipped. An* ESQUIRE, *carrying his sword and lance behind him.*[1]

COMMANDER.
Only thus far! I thank thee!—How stands all
I' the harbour? Is the galley there, full-rigged
To sail?

SQUIRE.
She only waits the trumpet-blast
To start; for favouring blows the wind, praise God!

COMMANDER.
Praise God, say'st thou? God mend it!—Give them me,
I still can carry lance myself—now go!
        [*Takes sword and lance from his hands.*
            Exit ESQUIRE.
        (*Alone; approaching Hugo's statue.*)
Well, ancient Hugo! my foreboding soul
Warns me we meet from this day forth no more;
Farewell!—Thy grey disciple ne'er again
Shall see thy face! It hath me many a time,
When blackness lay before my soul, God mend it!
With magic power revived. This day they lead
To France thine aged son; there, boys will come
Deriding the old grey-beard's antique style
And bearing; nor shall them my trusty sword
Chastize, for now my arm has lost its nerve
And power! and therefore I have rather brought
To thee the sword. These seven deep notches here
        (*Showing them on the sword.*)

---

[1] Rule XXXI. "We grant unto each Knight only one esquire."—*Trans.*

Thou know'st them well; for always when I fought,
Thy spirit with me dwelt!
              [Lays the sword on the pedestal of the statue.
              Thou hast received
The better part of me:—the outer frame
Goes tottering still;—then leave old Hugo not
To make child's sport; but gather him to thee!
            (Advancing to the niche.)
And now unto the Mother of all Grace!
            [He draws back the curtain which veils the niche, and exposes to view a small Altar with a figure of Mary, which latter he addresses as follows.

Dost thou remember still how much I pledged,
Now sixty years ago, a lad of mettle,
To thee, and the beloved Queen, Lady Blanche,[1]
And all I vowed—I liv'd amongst you then,
An active Templar; wife, or child, or hearth,
All joyaunce that makes glad the heart of men,
I never had!—Only the double-Cross
Upon my mantle, and my trusty sword,
And she the royal lady of my heart,
And thou, the Lady and the Queen of Heaven,
(I cannot separate you each from each!)
Ye stilled within me thoughts of wife and child
(Which otherwise would oft have haunted me),
I was not satiated, God mend it!—yet
Content; in battle's heat, the strong man found
Love's guerdon. Now I am eighty past, God mend it!
Bald is this head; but loyally I've kept
My vow of seemliness and courtesy.
These wounds (*pointing to his head*), thou mind'st thee yet
    of them, I gained
Long since at Acca, fighting in thy cause,
When we were forced to evacuate, for aye,
The Saviour's land of marvels. I, with ten,
Last remnant of so many warriors true;
Ah, when we had thence embarked in our frail skiff

---

[1] Blanche of Castile, mother of St. Louis and Regent of France.—*Trans.*

For Cyprus, few were we[1] but with us went
The Lord's own strength! That time is over now,
Those ten are dust and ashes, yet God mend it!
Old Hugo still crawls slowly on the earth,
But can no more his prancing steed bestride,
Nor swing his shimmering lance. Thou gav'st it me
    (*Laying his lance upon the Altar.*)
And now take back again thy gift—God mend it!
I have been steward of it with perfect mind.
With perfect mind?—Nay, Holy Virgin, there
The old man lied! God mend it! No!—Fell not
Poor Robert?—O Mother! Can thy mantle's grace
Enfold and hide unreason's blemished face?
Yet ofttimes may thy servant, perchance, the right have
    done;
Accept the grey-haired sinner, for the love of thy dear Son!
    [*He kneels before the image of Mary and tries to pray.*

Enter ROBERT, *dressed as a secular Knight, unobserved by*
    COMMANDER HUGO, *who is deeply absorbed in
    his endeavour to pray.*

        ROBERT (*perceiving the* COMMANDER).
At last! He's here. He seems absorbed in prayer.
Shall I disturb him? How his silver'd head
Gleams in the rosy light of dawning day!
How curiously it shows reflected back
Upon the shafts of lapis lazuli!
How home-like all here seems to me, and yet
Estranged, depressing!
    (*Looking at the statue of André of Montbarry.*)
            Hast thou still thy scrip,

---

[1] After the loss of Jerusalem, Acca, now St. Jean d'Acre, became the metropolis of the Latin Christians, and the Templars exercised there one of the numerous independent commands by which the city had many sovereigns but no government. It was stormed by the Mamelukes, May 18, 1291. The convent-fortress of the Templars resisted three days longer; but the great Master was pierced with an arrow; and of five hundred knights only ten were left alive. The King of Jerusalem, the patriarch, and the great Master of the hospital effected their retreat to the shore; but the sea was rough and many were drowned before they could reach Cyprus.—*Gibbon*, ch. 59.—*Trans.*

Pilgrim? I too must wander. Shall the end
My pilgrimage awaiting, be like thine?
   (*Looking back again on the* COMMANDER.)
How fervently the old man yonder prays!
He draweth nigh his goal. Why melts this heart
Of mine with sadness never felt till now,
Not heretofore so careworn? Wherefore is't
Cold shudderings thrill through all my frame, as though
The spirits of the giant times of old
Were hovering round me in this spacious hall?
'Twould seem the marble forms took on them life;
Is this illusion? (*pointing to the statue of Hugo, founder of
  the Order.*)
     Hugo beckons me,
Holds out to me his banner! False conceit!
Vain-glorious dream, no more! Still he prays on,
The aged Grand-Commander! What would I
Not give for one kiss on those eyebrows grey,
One benediction from that hero hand!
Yet—No! Not now profaned by earthly griefs
That saintly spirit's quiet calm shall be!
Flee, sorrowing Robert, flee this land of rest!
And shalt thou win another yet, my soul?
   (*Looking at the statues of the Masters.*)
Obeys not subject nature man's control?
Ye smile, ye ancient Masters?—well and good!
Know I, too, am a man, ye giant brood!
Ye could create, and I?—I can renounce as surely,
And, freed from thrall, can reach, alone, my goal securely!

ASTRALIS *appears as a youth, dressed in bright blue, with a
  letter in her hand.*

ASTRALIS (*approaching* ROBERT, *just as he is turning round to
  go out by the door, with disguised voice*).
Greeting to thee, Sir Robert of Heredon!

    ROBERT.
Who calls me?

   ASTRALIS (*offering him the letter*).
  Read, and what thou readest, mark!

ROBERT (*looking at her in astonishment*).
Thy name is?—

ASTRALIS.
Astralon.

ROBERT.
I had a dream
A while ago, a dream that looked like thee!

ASTRALIS.
Thou shalt not dream! Haste to the harbour, where
E'en now the ship from Scotland waits for thee.
Wake up! Expect to see me in thy home!
[*Exit quickly.*

ROBERT (*looking after her calmly*).
Wake up? I *am* awake! A curious note! (*Examining it*).
The address is Scotch, my mother-tongue. The form
A pentagon, the wax and letters green;
The seal a quartered field, whereon I see
A lion, a fox, an ape, and—as it seems—
A sparrow-hawk the fourth. Astonishing!
'Tis almost like a fable. Let us see!
"Brave Scot! who art no Templar Knight, and yet
Art guardian of the Temple! Much that now
Shows dimly will be manifest, one day.
Go home in peace; but on the eighteenth day
Of the third moon in the twice seventh year,
In the century the four and fiftieth,[1]
Of the Revealing, be at Paris by
The Temple-tower,[2] and rescue the red Cross

---

[1] *i.e.*, 14th year of the 14th century, 1314; leaving 4,000 years before Christ. Molay died in 1314.

[2] The Temple, formerly the head-quarters of the Knight Templars in Paris, consisted of two buildings—the Palace, facing the Rue du Temple, usually occupied by one of the Princes of the Blood; and the Tower, standing behind the Palace. The Tower was a square building, with a round tower at each corner and a small turret on one side, usually called the Tourelle. Louis XVI. and his family were imprisoned in the Tower.—MME. CAMPAN'S *Life of Marie Antoinette*. Annexe to chap. xi.—*Trans.*

From midst the flames. Subject to change are form
And colour, but the primal element
Abides eternally.¹ We wait for thee
In the green Valley of Peace, where stilled and mute
For ever is the royal lion's roar."

                 [*He folds up the letter and gazes thought-
                  fully before him, then makes his exit
                  quickly from the hall.*

COMMANDER (*rising from before the Altar where he has hitherto
    knelt, and for the last minute only has been able to pray,—
    much exhausted by this long effort of prayer*).
Thank thee, pure maid, that thus thy grace did'st manifest.
I ne'er in my whole life have been revived so throughly,
Yet am I tired, so tired. Prayed I? Was my prayer blest?
No!—Speechless, void of thought, in air I floated; truly,
Methought a suckling babe, I pressed my mother's breast,
And shuddering through my frame, a second birth dawned
    newly!
If 'twere indeed a prayer, I might believe it nearly;
For a man has done with weeping when he can pray sin-
    cerely.

                 [*He looks out of the windows, down on the
                  valley, from which the morning mists
                  are beginning to rise; after a pause,
                  during which he has in some measure
                  recovered from his extreme exhaus-
                  tion, he is sufficiently revived to open
                  the side-door leading into the cloister.*

Is this not Molay, coming from the cloister?
            (*To* MOLAY, *who comes in.*)
Astir so soon, old boon-companion mine?

                MOLAY.
Aye! For the last time I've been watering

---

¹ It is a matter of no essential importance where or how the Sun
selects a temple of flesh to contain his godhead. The confraternity of
the Valley of Peace aim at preserving the pristine element of truth, so
that, on the destruction of the Templars, it may resurge like the Phoenix
from its ashes, and this task is to be entrusted to the Scottish Knight,
Sir Robert of Heredom.—*Trans.*

The Tartar, comrade of my fighting days;
And I've been up the mountain. Brother Hugo,
How good for him, who's hastening towards his grave,
It is to contemplate the wide expanse
Of all the bright, free, living world of God,
Where all seeds sown to such fair harvest come!
And those seeds, Hugo, we too have been sowing,
They are not lost?

COMMANDER.
Be that as the Lord will!
I question not; God grant a happy end!

MOLAY.
Thou'rt come forth of thy cell full early.

COMMANDER.
Yes!
The howling of the storm, the thunder's roll
By two o'clock had driven me out, God mend it!
Sure never have I known so wild a night;
'Twas e'en as though the foul fiend with his knaves
Were playing skittles.

MOLAY.
God has fore-ordained
The skittle he shall strike; the servant plays;
The Lord doth win the game. Brother, thou'rt arm'd!
(*As his glance falls on the* COMMANDER'S *armour.*)

COMMANDER.
Comrade! I must confess myself to thee;
'Tis foolish, but, God mend it! everything
Just now's a chari-vari!—And so I thought,
My Brother; " Thou shouldst show thyself once more,
In all thy pomp of arms, to these thine old
Companions here; for all too soon thou'lt be
Surrounded by a young and frivolous world."
Therefore I went, and dedicated sword
And lance to old Hugh, and the Holy Maid;
And then—deride me not, my comrade,—then

It seemed to me the blank unlighted eyes
Were softening to me!

MOLAY.
                    Spare me!—I have need
Of strength to-day: the stately Master's garb
But scantly clothes my aching human heart!
Sails Robert yet towards his native land?

COMMANDER.
Surely the young man will take leave; but, Molay,
Believe me I am much forewarned of Robert
That God has greatness yet in store for him.
Whilst here before the gracious form I knelt,
It happened that I in the crystal looked
Whereon shines back the Virgin's radial crown;
Sudden, it seemed, I in that mirror saw
Our Robert, and by his side, an angel, garbed
In heavenly blue. And they were radiant both
As though the Light of Glory lit them up.[1]
I saw him also in my dreams last night,
Girt up as simple handicraftsmen are;
When suddenly he stood before me there,
In form gigantic; with his head he touched
High Heaven, and with his feet earth's central point:
Embraced the world from east to west, and cried
"Nature irradiates and serves the Pure."

MOLAY.
It was a dream!—

COMMANDER.
            No doubt, but yet, God mend it!
I'd fain interpret it!—

---

[1] This crystal was probably of the family of the Magic Crystals which have been so widely esteemed for purposes of divination from East to West. Held in honour by the Babylonians of old, they command even now the reverence of the people in the Hebrides and West of Scotland. (See "From the Hebrides to the Himalayas," by C. F. Gordon Cumming.)
    Mr Hugo, who really saw the reflected forms of Robert and Astralis (Astralon), was not surprised to think he beheld a vision.—*Trans.*

MOLAY.
               Oh, we dream all!
But our capacity for dreaming proves
To me the existence of those Holy Heights
Which waft down cooling breezes on the waste,
When the Sirocco dries our juices up.

                    COMMANDER.
I will go look for him, lest he escape
Without leave taking!

                    MOLAY.
                    Good! I'll wait for thee,
Till to the port we go.   [*Exit* COMMANDER.
             (*Alone.*) They tarry long!
             [*A knocking is heard at a small door concealed by the Altar of Mary.*
Ah, there they are!—Come in, ye who elect!
             [*He draws the hood of his mantle over his head, and locks the principal door.*

The PRESBYTER, PHILIP, Brother of the Garden, *the* MARSHAL, *the* DRAPER, *the* STANDARD-BEARER, *and* CLAUS RÖSNER [1] *come in from the concealed door. All have drawn the hoods of their mantles or frocks over their heads; each carries a short blood-red sword, on a girdle to match, which, as he comes in, each hangs round his neck.*

             MOLAY (*going in among them*).
Place yourselves in the figure!—

                    PRESBYTER (*interrupting him*).
                              Brother Leader,
Your leave to speak!

---

[1] They form with Molay, the mystic number seven. In the time of the Crusade, seven Syriac Christians who had inherited esoteric doctrine from the Essenes, received protection from the Templars and confided to them their secrets.—FROST, *Secret Societies.*—*Trans.*

MOLAY.
Speak!—

PRESBYTER.
Thus the Spirit spake
Within me: that the second Brother Watchman (*pointing
to* PHILIP)
Was not collected in himself to-day. (*To* PHILIP, *sharply
observing him.*)
Art thou so?

PHILIP (*after a pause*).
No!

PRESBYTER (*with mild seriousness*).
Why, then, disturb not thou
The office of last unction!

PHILIP (*in a similar tone*).
I thank thee.
[*He takes his sword from round his neck,
and hands it to* MOLAY.

MOLAY (*embracing him*).
My Brother, God invigorate thee!   [PHILIP *goes out.*

MOLAY (*to the* MARSHAL).
To-day,
Thou must be second Watchman, in the place
Of Philip.

MARSHAL.
There can be no office: we
Are not full seven!

PRESBYTER.
Therefore have I brought
My youngest choir-boy, whom I've taught to say

The Holy Urim-Thummim[1] which may be named
By the youngest of us only. He is ready.
Shall he lead us to-day, Brethren?

MOLAY.
Adept,
A child is, since so newly come from seeing;
Bring then the boy here, that he us may lead!
[*The* PRESBYTER *goes out, and returns
immediately, bringing in a Chorister
five years of age, with eyes bandaged,
and places him before* MOLAY.

MOLAY (*laying hands on the child's head*).
The Lord be with thee!

The OTHERS.
And with thy spirit!

MOLAY
(*To the others, after he has hung* PHILIP'S *sword round the
Child's neck*).
Now,
Form yourselves in the figure! Raise the Cross!

---

[1] The Urim and Thummim worn by the Jewish High Priest inside the breastplate, on his ephod, whenever he went in before the Lord, may probably best be rendered in English as " Light and Perfection ; " by some it has been rendered " Perfect Illumination." Scripture represents it as divinely oracular; and some have thought the Urim to reside in the rock-crystal (or diamond) of the breastplate. The old Grand-Commander imagined himself to have seen a vision in the crystal on, or above, the altar of Mary (Act VI. Scene 2), in front of which these mysterious proceedings of the Templars are taking place. The high attributes of their mummy or teraph-head, mentioned a little further on, recalls the further scriptural fact that, in some cases of deflection from the established religious order, we find the ephod connected not with the Urim but with the Teraphim, which in the day of Laban, if not earlier, had been conspicuous in Aramaic worship. (Jud. xvii. 5-18, xiv. 20, Hosea iii. 4.) The Teraphim were probably unauthorized substitutes for the Urim, and used in unholy forms of divination. (See " Dict. of the Bible.") Gottfried complains (Act IV.) that they (the Templars) are called Necromancers, and he thinks himself there is something not quite as it should be about their teraph-head. — *Trans.*

> (*The* ADEPTS, *arranged whom the* PRESBYTER
> *leads the boy into the fifth place, form
> themselves into a special figure, of
> which the* LEADER *and the two* WATCH-
> MEN *form the three ends.*'[1] *Then they
> lift up their small swords in the form
> of a great Cross.*

LEADER.

In the name of Him, the One and Everlasting,
I open in the morning these our halls!—
You know the King who built them! Name his signet!

Second WATCHMAN.

Dimension!

First WATCHMAN.

Area!

LEADER.

Boundary! The halls

Rest. And now let your swords be lowered again!

> [*All step out of the figure, and let their
> swords fall back again on their breasts.
> The First* WATCHMAN *leads the*
> YOUNGEST *before the Altar of Mary,
> leaving him kneeling there with folded
> hands, and returns to the* ADEPTS.

LEADER.

We come together, we seven Adepts, to-day
For the last time,—so saith to me the Spirit,—
To execute a task of great concern.
Which partly I've informed you of already.
The time is short; the deed needs haste and silence.

---

[1] As the Adepts in this transaction, which they hold an important, entirely forget their own personality themselves, neither will the author remember it on the present occasion, but will call Molay (now as appearing as Master) the Leader; the Presbyter, the First; the Marshal, the Second Watchman; the Draper, Standard-Bearer, and Rhoser by the general term Adepts, and the child, simply the Youngest.

I go to France. You, some of you stay here.—
Pure though our meaning be, our duty is,
To arm ourselves with foresight, and expose
To Envy's sight no least weak point whereby
Contempt might be upon our Order thrown.
Therefore by counsel of the enlightened three,
Who in the Temple are, besides ourselves,
Adept,—Prior Guido, Peter of Boulogne,
Adam of Valincourt—and in the name
Of fourteen Masters who, outside the Temple,
Are yet Adept upon the earth's expanse,—
I am minded to commit unto the flames
Some several of those writings which reveal
The Order's secrets and might serve to feed
The envious ill-will of the enemy.
The Brothers three, already named, at Paris,
Are of like mind; these letters are from them.
        [*He gives to each of the three eldest*
        WATCHMEN *a letter; they give the*
        writings back to him after looking
        them over.
You, too, deliberately I ask again,
Do you approve it?

        First WATCHMAN.
        Under the condition
The Holy Things be not destroyed, we do!

        The LEADER.
(*Raising the flagstone of a vault which lies before Hugo's
    statue, and bringing up a chest from the cavity that is
    beneath it, and placing it on the ground.*)
Stored in this coffer are the Order's books.
(*To one of the younger* ADEPTS, *after he has opened the box.*)
Brother, their titles read![1]

---

[1] Sir Gerard de Caus gave information, according to the French action-at-law concerning the investigation decreed against the Order, that Molay previously to his leaving Cyprus, burnt the most important documents of the Order, and took some of them with him.—*Trans.*

ADEPT (*reading*).
          "Rules of the Order
Of Temple-Guardians of Jerusalem."

THE LEADER (*taking the book out of his hand, and closing it
          again, as he lays it upon the pedestal*).
I'll not take this,—Pure as the Master's word
This book is—Brother, take a key and keep
It safe.—(*Gives the* Second WATCHMAN *a key.*)
          The others I will keep myself.

          ADEPT (*reading*).
The same, a copy.

          LEADER (*to the* Second WATCHMAN).
          Take it, we'll leave it here.

          ADEPT.
(*Taking another book out of the chest and opening it, reads.*)
"Veracious Record, how by Thomas Berald,
The four and twentieth of the Temple Masters,
The knowledge of the one God was restored,
And, darkened by no shadow of the Cross,
The Moon shed light upon men's path of old."

          LEADER.
We've ceased to use it, and to younger men
This Light might prove an *ignis-fatuus*.   (*To the* ADEPT.)
Bring me the fire, go kindle it at the lamp!
          [*The* ADEPT *advances in front of the Altar
               of Mary, takes a chafing-dish which
               stands upon it, kindles the coal at the
               lamp which hangs down in front of
               the altar, then comes back again with
               the burning coal in the pan and
               places it before the* LEADER.
LEADER (*taking the last-named book and holding it over the
          pan of coals, to the other* ADEPTS).
If you consent?

First WATCHMAN.
Be it reduced to ashes!—
[*The* LEADER *throws it in the flames.*

ADEPT (*taking out another book, reads*).
"Concerning Baphom, the Illuminator."

LEADER (*taking possession of it*).
Analogous contents; then shall it share
A similar fate?—

WATCHMAN.
So be it; we are content.
[*The* LEADER *throws it into the flames.*

ADEPT (*takes out another book, and reads*).
"Touching three Masters, Moses, Christ"—the third
I cannot read, for it is writ in cipher.

LEADER (*to the two* WATCHMEN).
You two both know the name?

Both WATCHMEN.
We do.

LEADER.
                          Then may
I take it?

First WATCHMAN.
Be it trusted to thy care!

ADEPT (*brings out a very small book, and reads*).
"The Star out of the East."

Both WATCHMEN (*both together hastily snatching at it*).
                    On no account
Must this be burnt!

LEADER (*taking it*).
             Could I so dissipate
The Diamond? (*he sticks it in his girdle.*)

In my girdle here safe-stowed
I'll guard it, but you have my knightly word
That I or an Elect will bring it back. (*After he has covered
    up the brasier, containing the burnt papers.*)
The writing dies, the eternal symbol lives!

            ADEPT (*searching in the coffer*).
There's something gleams like metal underneath.

        LEADER (*springing on him and thrusting him back*).
There let it lie!

            First WATCHMAN.
                Where that book is, this must
Be also.

            LEADER.
(*To the* ADEPTS, *pointing to the chest and its remaining contents*).
            I will take with me to France
The coffer.

            Second WATCHMAN (*astonished*).
            What? the silver vessels and jewels,
The candlesticks, the palm-leaves also?

            LEADER.
                        All!

All the ADEPTS (*except the leader and* First WATCHMAN).
Wilt thou despoil the Holy Things?

            LEADER.
                    Not so!
But guard them carefully till happier times.[1]
            [*Indicating the* First WATCHMAN.
The Watchman knows I have full powers.

---

[1] De Molay took with him to the palace of the Templars in Paris the chest, or chests, of the Order—twelve mules' load of gold and silver. The treasure was put away in the Templar vaults.—FROUDE, *Good Words*, July, 1866.—*Trans.*

First Watchman.
                    He has.

Leader.
(To an Adept, *handing to him the coffer, after he has placed in it the two books preserved from destruction, and carefully locked everything up.)*
Thou'lt put the coffer secretly on board
The ship; thy head stands surety for it!

The Adept.
(As he takes the coffer and hides it under his garment.)
                    Brother,
I am Adept!

Leader.
            There only now remains
One thing.
            [*He pulls out a slide which is in the pedestal under Hugo's statue, brings out of the opening thus made apparent a mummy-head crowned and wrapped in a golden veil, and shows it to the Knights.*
            This head. Its twofold portraiture
Ye know—the Fallen, as to the wholly blind
We show it, and the Arisen, as to the half
Illuminate.[1] I love these mysteries not.
They are, how pure soe'er their origin,
The source of much abuse, which I intend
To regulate at our next general Chapter,
With others of like nature.—Yet the veil
Is o'er *our* eyes no longer, and this head
Shows us, without an effigy, the dear

---

[1] Meaning, apparently, as Baphometus to those without dawn of insight, and as the Arisen Prince of Victory (see Act I. Scene 1) to those with partial insight; while to the fully illuminate, he shows the relic of the King,—be he called Solomon, or Hiram, or Dis, or whatever be his Masonic-theosophic name,—whose glorified essence is the Vision or Idol of the Promised Land, to be sought, till found, by the Pure. (See Act V. Scene 2.)—*Trans.*

Remainder of the King geometrical,
Baptized with wisdom, beautified through strength,
Friend of the Lord, who showed Himself to him,
And granted him the signet of his power.
Kiss him for the last time!

     [*The* ADEPTS *bow low. The* LEADER *holds
     out the hand for each one to kiss.*

     So!—now to earth
I yield him till that seed in honour rise
Which we have sown in bitterness and pain.

     [*He lowers the head into the open vault,
     which he covers with the flagstone.
     This transaction, in which he is as-
     sisted by some of the younger* ADEPTS,
     *is performed in complete silence. The
     remaining* ADEPTS *look on with hands
     crossed over the breast, and reverently
     bowed heads. Solemn pause.*

   MOLAY (*pointing to the stone*).
So, rest thee here for ever!—But, ye swear
That none shall henceforth lift the stone again!—

   First WATCHMAN (*sharply and earnestly to him*).
Hadst thou, no less, for this momentous step
Authority?

     LEADER.
  I had.
(*He says something in his ear; then to the others.*)
     What now I do
I will account for in the Valley.

     [*The* ADEPTS *bow reverently—Holding
     out to them that side of his mantle on
     which is the Cross.*
     Swear!

   The ADEPTS (*each laying two fingers on the Cross*).
We swear!

     LEADER (*to the youngest* ADEPT).
  Give to the lamp its own!

The Leader!
(*To the* First Watchman.) Admit

[*The* Adept *takes the pan of coals and carries it back to the Altar: then returns. The* First Watchman *goes to the* Youngest, *who has all this time been kneeling at the Altar, and leads him with eyes still blindfolded into the group of* Adepts.

Leader.
Form the figure!—Raise the Cross!—
[*The Seven* Adepts *place themselves, with their swords in the figure as before.*
In the name of Him the One and Everlasting
I hereby close the Halls for the last time!
How is the Valley's Gate named?

Second Watchman.
Brightness!

First Watchman.
Depth!

Second Watchman.
(*To the* First Watchman *and the* Leader.)
Tell us the Valley's name!

First Watchman.
Not I!

Leader.
Nor I.
[*The* First Watchman *conducts the* Youngest *to the* Leader's *place. All kneel down, except the* Youngest, *to whom approach first the* Leader, *then the* First, *and lastly the* Second Watchman.

The YOUNGEST (*says a trisyllabic word in the ear of each of the three elder ADEPTS, then says aloud to the three younger*).
Love!

LEADER.
What doth that mean?

The YOUNGEST (*in a faltering babble*).
—I in me— we are—
Existence!

[*With these words the CHILD closes the Halle. The rest stand up.*]

PRESBYTER.
(*Confounded, as are all the others, by the formula, hitherto unknown to them, which has been stammered out by the CHILD, half aside to him.*)
'Twas not so I taught it thee!

The CHILD (*with infantile smile*).
Gottlieb can't say it any other way![1]

MOLAY (*as well as CLAPS regarding with delight the CHILD who has thus fraternised with them, aloud and distinctly to the rest*).
HE help us to the Valley!—The kiss of peace!
(*They embrace one another.*)
Pray we that His own Spirit's light may in our souls be shown,
That so the Temple's Lord may to the Temple be made known!

[*The two Elders, namely, the PRESBYTER and the MARSHAL, led by GOTTLIEB, whose eyes still remain blindfolded, go softly through the side-door hidden by the Altar, through which they are followed by the three younger, namely,*

---

[1] That is to say, the Presbyter had taught the Child the customary formula of the Adepts, much resembling the above formula and differing from it but very slightly in the expressions; yet, through this slight variation, quite different from it in the sense and in the result: which formula of the Adepts the Child, newly come from seeing, could not repeat.

     the DRAPER, the STANDARD-BEARER,
     and ROSNER, all having first taken off
     their swords and hidden them under
     their garments.

    MOLAY (calling after RÖSNER).

Claus!

    [CLAUS comes in again. MOLAY throws back
    the hood of his mantle, goes to Hugo's
    statue, takes out of the opening in its
    pedestal a paper with seven seals, hides
    it under his mantle, then having
    pushed in again the slide of the
    pedestal, comes up to CLAUS.

  MOLAY (to CLAUS, half smiling, half serious).
If so be I die, wilt thou still live?

      CLAUS.

Not willingly.

      MOLAY.
   Claus! thou'rt Illuminate!

      CLAUS.

But human still!

      MOLAY.
    What gave I thee, when first
Thou cam'st to Cyprus?

      CLAUS.
     How could I forget
Thy goodness, ever?—

      MOLAY.
    'Tis not that!—Forget
My part in it, but hold fast what is thine!

      CLAUS.
A brave wife, healthy children, these are mine.[1]

---

[1] Rule LV. We permit you to have married brothers in this manner; let both the man and his wife grant, from and after their death, their

MOLAY (*impressively*).
God sent thee these, and He can take them back!

CLAUS.
My joy is, that I can provide for them;
For this, I owe your generous kindness thanks,
Which, when I came here, a poor working man,
In search of better fortune such as ne'er
At home in Germany had smiled on me,
Received me, educated, set me up!

MOLAY.
Enough of that!—What hast thou learnt of me?
Naught but to earn bread for thyself and thine?

CLAUS (*confused*).
Brother!

MOLAY.
What?—Polished I thy Square for naught
But that thou shoul'dst thy private angle measure?
I grant 'tis good and regular.

CLAUS (*gladly*).
Aye, is't not?

MOLAY.
Each in its own niche all is ranged within
Thy cottage. With thy wife and children, thou
An Order form'st which shames the Temple league;
Thou art—Friend! very few achieve so much,—
Almost thou'rt perfect,—as regards thyself!

CLAUS.
It is thy work!

MOLAY.
But only as regards
respective portions of property, and whatever more they acquire in after life, to the unity of the common chapter; and in the interim, let them exercise an honest life, labour to do good to the brethren; but they are not permitted to appear in the white habit and white mantle.—*Truss.*

Thyself. Thou'rt far yet from the goal,—a good,
A well-trained—bungler—

              CLAUS (*naïvely*).
                  Were I thee!

              MOLAY.
                            What more
Am I? Yet higher is my aim than thine!
He who but seeks to garnish his own hut
Is but a bungler! Gave I thee thy cot,
Plied'st thou thy tools thereon, but to remain
A bungler, and build up no solid house
For all mankind?—

              CLAUS.
                Fain would I—though 'tis hard,—
And yet, because of thee, I fain would part
From wife and child, and go with thee to France.

              MOLAY.
Ah, bungler!—why should'st thou pull down to build?
Art thou the master-builder? Scarcely thou
Art journeyman! Leave each man his; perform
Thine own.

              CLAUS.
        What is it?

              MOLAY.
                The red Cross perhaps
May fall; but even if a thing be like
To One, the Eternal; yet it lets itself
This way or that be handled, by who would
Lay fast hold on it.

              CLAUS.
          Do I comprehend
Thy meaning?

              MOLAY.
        I believe thou dost. Thou knowest

My estimation of the coloured Cross,
As also of the Knights.

CLAUS.
                    Yes; thou dost oft
Throw in one pot so many things, one looks
To see a hotch-potch come of it, yet when
The broth is ready, it is nutritive.

MOLAY.
Thou art a handicraftsman, Brother Claus,
A German true; ye Germans apprehend
Slowly indeed but surely, and 'tis well!
Dear Claus, I die; the Order too, perhaps,—
But I undoubtedly!

CLAUS (*with intense pain*).
                    Wilt thou destroy
Me utterly?

MOLAY (*smiling*).
            Poor fool!—a testament
Is not yet absolutely death! (*Seriously.*) I gave
The Knowledge to thee, seeing thou could'st act;
Thou stridest forth in action, so no less
In Wisdom surely! The red Cross—the Knights!
A colour red is; it can be wash'd out!
A Knight, a Chevalier, is one who rides,
But like his poor old horse, goes lame at last!
E'en though the Cross be shatter'd, there remain
Yet fragments doing duty for the whole!
And as for knights, there's no great need of them,
For who knows how to use his arms and legs,
He has been knighted by Queen Nature.
(*After a pause, during which he holds* CLAUS *with a fixed
    gaze, looking into his eyes with intense and increasing
    scrutiny.*)
                                Claus!
What wilt thou do? If I should die, what part
Wilt thou perform? Thou canst do much! Be mine

This solace, that I leave behind me one,
At least, who's not a blunderer! My Robert—

CLAUS.
Robert is more than I am!

MOLAY.
Truly, yes!
But only towards the esoteric works
His strength divine, thine outwards; for which cause
Thou art initiated, not he.

CLAUS.
And thou
Could'st cast him out!

MOLAY.
And thereby broke my heart,
But justice was maintained. Lovest thou him?

CLAUS.
Not as my Anna, not so much as thee,
Far less; but more than any other man.

MOLAY (*gladly*).
Praise be to God!—the morning dawneth. Rösner!
Is Robert highly gifted?

CLAUS.
Yes.

MOLAY.
Is any
Within the Order comparable to him?

CLAUS.
Not one!

MOLAY.
Lives he in vain?

CLAUS.
                    No single stone
Of a foundation lieth there in vain!

MOLAY.

(*Regarding his disciple with augmenting enthusiasm.*)
I feel God mediates between thee and me!
(*Sensibly.*) My Robert, Brother, ere I cast him out,
Already had outgrown the Temple-Order:
Long since, the Temple-Master was to him
As nought! I am a saint to him, remote
From him, and though the halo of a saint
I could forego, yet so 'tis well for him,
And well for—me; for, Brother, hard it is
To die without an heir! Poor Robert goes
To Scotland now, and goes with God! Will God
Bring me and him to realize my aim?
Him also?—But should we with idle hand
In bosom thrust, look on?—Look on; no more,
And take no part? Not such God's will; 'tis true
He doeth all things of Himself, but we
Are placed here to co-operate with him!
Thou art adept, my Römer: Templars may
Be brought to nought, even the Illuminate;
But all shall not, please God,—they shall not all!
In Cyprus thou'lt remain—deny me not!
My death, not thine, can profit,—therefore live
To merit it! Our Halls in Edinburgh
Thou knowest, and the key,—make use of it!
Should this our Order, fall, and—as I have
Deserved because of it—should I too fall
A sacrifice for it, guard then that young
Tree I have planted in the North, that so
It may, fruit bearing, over-shade the world,'
And not in vain the gardener may have lived.—

[1] The Rose-Croix of Heredon, or Heredom, is one of the degrees of Scotch Masonry. It was established first at Icolmkill, then at Kilwinning, where the King of Scotland presided in person as Grand Master. See *Thuileur de l'Ecossisme du rit ancien, dit accepté*, p. 132.
In the degree of the Knight of Palestine, substituted by the Chevalier de St. Martin in the place of Rose-Croix, is celebrated the Institution of

CLAUS.
In vain! (*striking hands with* MOLAY).
My brother, I will live!

MOLAY (*looking up thankfully to heaven*).
I knew
That well—My Rösner's care will grow me flowers.
[*Draws the sealed paper from under his mantle and hands it to* RÖSNER.
There is my testament; the hieroglyphs
Thou comprehendest; nothing more is needed.
(*Imploringly.*) Thou wilt protect both it and Robert?

CLAUS.
Yes,
God helping!

MOLAY.
So my work survives, and I
Am satisfied. Brother, the parting kiss!
Thou weep'st?—Hast thou anew forgot the Square?

CLAUS (*kissing away* MOLAY's *tears*).
Art thou, then, iron?

MOLAY.
My aim is so to be!
Greet wife and child.—Whilst they are thine—be theirs.
God leaves them to thee just so long, no more,
As thou art blessed in their possession.—Go!

the Order of the Templars. This degree is *censé* to draw its origin from the Crusades. The Master represents Godfrey of Bouillon. The password is *Dieu-le veut*, the Templars' war-cry. The 27th degree of Scotch Masonry is called Grand-Commander of the Temple, or Sovereign Commander of the Temple of Jerusalem. Ibid. p. 196.

This degree is not to be confounded with the Order of modern Templars. Ibid. p. 199.

The 30th degree of Kadosch, though only the 30th, must be regarded as *the real end* of Scotch Masonry, as it is the *ne plus ultra* of Templar Masonry. It commemorates the abolition of the Templar Order by Philip the Fair and the Pope Clement V.; and the death of the last Grand-Master, James Molay, who perished in the flames, March 11, 1314. Ibid.—*Trans.*

[*Rises in gem. The* MASTER *reviews himself after his strong emotion, by looking out into the valley, which is already flooded by the crimson of dawn. Pause.*

Thank God! the important duty all is done;
The Lord may call me now, for I am ready!—

COMMANDER HUGO *limps wearily in.*

COMMANDER.
Robert is off already—gone without
Even taking leave of me, me who—God mend it!

MOLAY (*wearily*).
Already gone!

Enter CHARLOT (*to* MOLAY).
The Brother-Messengers,
They whom your Grace sent lately to the King,
And to the Master of the Hospital,
Are back again, and wait without.

MOLAY (*to* CHARLOT).
Hast thou
Been to the harbour?

CHARLOT.
Yes, the people throng
Down there in crowds to see you once again!
All fear you will return to them no more.

MOLAY.
Kind souls!—Good sooth, there's none that curses me?

CHARLOT.
Most eyes were wet, dismay is general!

Enter GOTTFRIED.
The Watch sends word the hurricane this night
Has from the tower thrown down the Cross; also,
'Tis said the vault sent dismal wailings up!—

MOLAY (*annoyed*).
Silence! Secure the Cross, and warn the Watch
Not to disturb the people with such tales. [*Exit* GODFREY.
(*To* CHARLOT.) Now introduce the Brother-messengers!
[*Exit* CHARLOT.

Enter KNIGHTS *in coats of mail.*

MOLAY (*to the* First KNIGHT).
What bring'st thou from the King?

First KNIGHT.
I was denied
Admission to his presence;[1] but his minion
Count Lusignan, to whom I in your name
Commended the protection of the Temple,
Replies to you—these are his actual words:
"Do thou defend the Temple for thyself!
You'll find King Henry will protect the Crown,
For so 'tis meet."

MOLAY.
Denied admission! Such
Reply to me! (*Aside.*) Dost thou already scorn
Th' old Lion! (*To the other* KNIGHT.)
My Brother of the Hospital,
What doth he say?

The Other KNIGHT.
He bade me greet your Grace,
And charged me with this letter to deliver
Into your hands.

MOLAY (*to the two* KNIGHTS).
Go! [*Exeunt the two* KNIGHTS.
" Fulke de Villaret
To James de Molay—Not thy friend am I,
Yet frank plain-speaking well becomes a Knight.
Molay! Go not to France.—I also have
My summons thither, but I do not care

---

[1] There was a continual tendency to jealousies and disputes between the Templars and the King of Cyprus, who viewed with distrust their increase and power.—*Trans.*

To pay the score. Dost not thou know the cowl?
Sleek it is outwardly, but hides within
A tiger's teeth; creep under it and see
If thou shalt come with whole skin out again!
I'm not that sort: but from the Turk, God willing,
I shall recover Rhodes. And, if thou wilt,
Look in upon me there and dine with me!"
    (*Folding up the letter and putting it in his bosom*).
Unquiet, headstrong man!

          COMMANDER.
                The old soldier's right,
God mend it! My own head is in a state
Of marvellous perturbation. I foresee
Much detriment from this beginning!

          MOLAY.
                    God
Begins, not we. When many cross-roads lie
Before us tending divers ways and we
Doubt which to choose, He sends us Duty then,
A guide that ne'er misleads; and we will go!

          COMMANDER.
Well!—to the harbour I will go before,
And wait thee there.   [*Exit*.

        Enter GREGER.
                The old man with the lute
Is nowhere to be found!

        MOLAY (*Aside, looking up to Heaven*).
                Should the end come,
Oh, might I be the victim, one for all!

        Enter A SOLDIER (*quickly*).
The guard has just announced that Brother Noffo
And Prior Heribert of Montfaucon,[1]
Have broke from prison.—

---

[1] The Templar (in Masonry) sees in "the three murderers of Hiram" (the Tyrian sculptor and engraver, called metaphorically "the Architect

MOLAY (*shocked and alarmed*).
                    Noffo! In God's name
Pursue him!—Yet, no, stop!—For liberty
May bring him punishment or emendation!
Heribert too!—(*Aside.*) Alas! how fiercely stings
An injury done that cannot be repaired!

Enter CHARLOT.
A favouring wind invites us out to sea.

MOLAY.
Then in God's name unfurl our banner free;
Peal bells; with song and music greet this day,
Our last in Cyprus!—To our goal, away!
            [*Exit quickly; the rest follow him.*

SCENE III.

Harbour, the sea in the background; on the left, on the shore, the Castle, whereon waves the flag of the Order. An armed warder with a trumpet, stands on the battlement. A red glow suffusing the sky announces the approaching sunrise. The bells sound from the distance, faintly at first, then louder. People of every age and sex throng the shore in the background. Amongst them, CLAUS *with his wife and two children, a boy and a girl from four to five years old.*

A WOMAN.
Are they not yet in sight?

of the Temple of Solomon" whose murderers are said to have stood outside the doors of the Temple to take his life) Squin de Florian, Noffodei, and the *Unknown*, on whose depositions Philip the Fair accused the Order before the Pope; or else, (besides) the *three abominable ones*, Philip the Fair, Clement the Vth, and Noffodei.

Other degrees of Masonry substituted others (such as Judas, Caiaphas, and Pilate, murderers of Jesus).—*Thuileur de l'Ecossisme.*

Froude speaks of Squin (he calls him Esquin von Florian) as having been Prior of Montfaucon, in "Good Words," July, 1886.—*Trans.*

A Citizen.
    Not yet.

Another.
            The sun
Must soon be up.

A Youth.
    How clear and bright expand
The heavens after such an awful night!

A Citizen (*pointing out to sea*).
See yonder canvas? Even now lit up
By a bright sun-ray! 'Tis the ship which home
To Scotland carries Robert.

Another.
    They've expelled
Him from the Order.

A Third.
    Say you so? Alas!
The pity of it! Such a gallant Knight!

A Fourth.
He must be guilty of some grave offence;
For just is Molay, and would rather bear
A thousand ills himself than punish once.

An Old Man.
Lo there!—the oldest Knight, Sir Hugo comes,
With the two youngest stripling Knights.

A Sixth.
            How droops
His head upon his breast!

A Woman.
    'Tis certain he
Will never home return.

AN OLD MAN.
He's done much good.

CLAUS (*half Aside to* ANNE *his wife*).
See where he comes, Anne, whom we have to thank
For Molay's favour.

ANNE.
Oh, God bless him for it!
[CLAUS *presses to the front through the
crowd, with his wife and children
clinging to him.*

COMMANDER HUGO (*appears in the foreground fully armed,
supported by* FRANK *and* ADALBERT; *an Esquire goes
before him, carrying his helmet*).

COMMANDER (*to his companions*).
Stand still awhile, whilst I take breath. Flits not
A small star yonder on the far-off sea?

FRANK.
The ship of Scotland.

PEOPLE (*pressing forwards and crying out*).
Long live Father Hugo!

CLAUS (*kissing the* COMMANDER'S *hand*).
Sir Hugo, fare thee well!

ANNE (*doing the same, tears in her eyes, holding her
children by the hand*).
Will you not bless
These little ones once more?

LITTLE GIRL (*to the* COMMANDER, *naïvely clinging to him*).
Father, wilt thou
Bring me another necklace for the feast?

BOY (*pushing her away*).
Father, a lance for me!

COMMANDER (*to the Knights, who are supporting him*).
God mend it!—Come!
(*To the children who, at the command of their mother, have knelt down before him and embrace his knees.*)
God bless you, children. (*To the Knights.*) Come! I shame myself!
These old eyes swim with tears. Support me, guide me!
I cannot see at all! Come!
(*To the people as he goes away.*) God be with you!
   [*Staggers off, leaning on the two youngest Knights; the Esquire preceding them.*

OLD MAX.

The worthy Knight!
   [CLARA *retires into the background with his wife and children. The bells peal louder.*

First CITIZEN.
Hark! how the bells e'en now
Are pealing from the tower of St. John![1]
See ye yon dust-cloud? Now they're on the way!

A YOUTH.
Ah, yonder flutters now the red-Cross flag
Swayed by the morning breeze—a noble banner!

First CITIZEN.
Can ye not hear them sing? In order first
Advance the Priests, next come the Knights!

A GIRL.
                           Rose-hued
Their mantles white shine through the blush of morn.

---

[1] It does not seem quite clear what connection the Templars had with S. John Baptist. He was patron saint of the Knights of S. John (Hospitallers) of Jerusalem, but Dugdale (*Monasticon Anglicanum*) does not appear to mention the Knights Templars as being under the patronage of any Saint. Werner, however, connects them throughout with S. John, and the cognizance of the *Agnus Dei* which is seen all over the inside of the Temple Church, as well as carved over the gateway in Fleet Street, which gateway was rebuilt by Inigo Jones after the fire of London, would seem to confirm him.—*Trans.*

Second CITIZEN.
See just behind the Cross, bare-headed walks
The Master Molay,—see how sad he looks,
And yet most calm!

AN OLD WOMAN.
May God forgive me!—when
I look on him, I seem to see our Saviour!

OLD MAN.
Aye, and in truth a Saviour he has been
To us, good man!

First CITIZEN.
Hark! listen to the chant!
[*The tinkle of the mass-bell is heard, and
behind the scenes the hymn of the
approaching procession.*

HYMN.
And when misfortune's ravening sea
Would in its angry rage close o'er us,
The might of God will set us free,
And victory o'er the foe secure us;
Across our path she shines, a star,—
Pure maid, to whom we subject are;
And God is all our strengh.

[*During the singing of the three last lines,
the procession appears in solemn
order—viz., First, Musicians with
flutes and clarionets; after them,
Soldiers with lances, flanking the
procession on each side; Choir-boys
with small bells; Chaplain with small
banners of the Cross, and censers;
then all the others, so that the Elders
go last, all in pairs, next to them the
Standard-Bearer, carrying the great
white banner of the Order, on which
is the red Cross; the Knights in coats
of mail, also in pairs, and last of all
the seven elder and official Knights;*

*the Brother of the Garden, PHILIP
bearing MOLAY'S helmet; the Pres-
byter of the Order with the Holy
Cross,[1] lastly MOLAY in full armour,
all with uncovered heads. People
streaming behind him, and towards
him from the shore. All is imbued
with solemnity and calm. After the
procession has moved round the stage
in a half circle, they place themselves
in scenographic ranks,—right, the
Presbyter with the Cross; left, the
Knights; behind both, the Soldiers.
The intervening space between the
two rows in the background is
occupied by the people. MOLAY comes
forward alone into the centre, close
behind him the Standard-Bearer with
the waving banner of the Order.
MOLAY enforces silence by a gesture.
Music and singing cease; all the
Knights cover their heads. Solemn
pause.*

   MOLAY (*to the* STANDARD-BEARER).
Read out the proclamation!
    [*During the following proclamation,* CLAUS
    presses up to MOLAY *who gives him
    the Master's kiss.* CLAUS *hurries back
    to his wife and children; all this he
    does rapidly, and without looking up.*

STANDARD-BEARER (*half turned to the people, in a loud voice*).
    Cypriot Burghers!
If any of you have present claim or future
On James de Molay, of Jerusalem's Temple
Grand-Master, who this day departs for France,
Let him stand forth and fearlessly declare it!

[1] Which the Templars believed they possessed in the original, and
held this original in high honour; although precisely because, accordi ng
to their belief, they possessed it, they with reason esteemed lightly its
various multiform and spurious facsimiles.

THE WHOLE PEOPLE (*falling on their knees*).
Only thy blessing crave we, righteous lord!

MOLAY (*turning to the people and fervently blessing them*).
The peace of God be with you!

ASTRALIS (*crying out behind the scenes*).
Woe! ah, woe!
[*Movement among the people; all spring to their feet.*

MANY VOICES OF THE PEOPLE.
The crazy hermit-maiden! Keep her back!

ASTRALIS, the Emissary of the Valley.
(*Dressed in penitential robe of yellow hair, girdled with a cord, and barefooted. Her hair streams wildly over her shoulders; she carries in her hand a blood-red crucifix in the form of a sword of justice, and shrieks out, as she rushes in, inspired with holy frenzy, to the many who want to pursue and take hold of her,—in harrowing tones*)
Let no man touch me!—Sent I am and holy!
(*Pointing to* MOLAY *and the* KNIGHTS; *addressing the people with wild exultant laughter.*)
See ye the flame-wreaths circling round his head?
Hear ye the air-borne wailings, "Molay, Molay!"
And fiery tongues leap o'er their mantles—Ho!
Hence, to the funeral-pile! away, away! [*Exit.*

MOLAY (*faith-inspired—after a pause, during which his bystanders, of whom but few stand proof under the trial of the Order, and the greater number of whom succumb to it, give vent, some to their hopes, and some to their doubts, but all, excepting the Presbyter carrying the Cross, to their terror*).
God is my refuge.
(*Takes the banner from the Standard-Bearer and delivers it to the Marshal, saying to him lowdly and firmly*)
Take the banner, Marshal!
I shall demand it back from thee unstained,
As God will one day claim of thee thy soul!

[*Trumpet-blast from the warder on the
Castle. The rays of the sun, at that
moment risen, gild the battlements of
the Temple. The bells are again
heard pealing; the ship appears by
the shore manned by Longsword,
among them stand the Commander
and the Harper, and then begins a
soft music of flutes and harps, which
continues to play during* MOLAY's
speech.

(*Rapturously, with arms uplifted.*)
The call resounds!—The sun that mounts the sky
Is hailed by chimes, and harpers' melody.—
Come, Brothers! So from night our star shall soar;
I breathe sweet balms from Life's eternal shore!—

[*The Master* MOLAY *hastens to the ship,
following the Cross borne before him;
the banner and the flag of the Cross
are waved aloft, the Brothers make
their way through a confused multitude
to the shore, amid the shouts of the
people. They go on board. The
sound of bells and harps continues,
accompanied by the tender tones of*
EUDO's *lute, silenced at last as the
ship disappears in the distance.*

EPILOGUE.

Leave we the Templars now to go their way,
And ask, what is our special aim in view,
The while we read this book, or while we write it.
For if aright we read it, then we write it.
Reading an action is as much as writing,
But we must couple action with volition;
For action without will is no true action,
Is virtually, though often done, a non-act,
But to volition must belong clear Light!

When we are willed to read, to write a poem,
The world we would contemplate in the little,
That is, would look on mankind in the large;
We want the soul's sublimest sphere of Life.
The spirit *alone*, the heart *alone*, are dead;
Each lives but in its cognate essence,—Love!—
That sighs its life out in their warm embrace.
'Tis not this cosmic mystery of begetting,
The birth it is, Art watches o'er and paints.

Tho' circumscribed, of lofty origin,
It is the infant born of faith and joy,
And more,—the grandchild of the Deity.
Yet Love hath sent his children's child to man,
Who, made in Love's own image, and of himself
A token, yet requires a sign. Wherefore
Art cannot give, if Art to men would speak,
The Essence, whereof man himself but dreams,
But only, of Love's joys the external Sign.

All Art symbolically points to Love,
But yet the symbol, like mankind, is poor,

The lifeless letter and the barren word,
(Tho' they be living inspiration's mask)
Yet are they ever of the Sign but signs:
Art-plastic apes more truly outward form,
The essence, Melos' child more clearly shows;[1]
Yet are there points where form and essence meet
In close embraces; glances, sighs, and tears!

And how shall he who ventures tremblingly
Anigh the flowery fields of holy Art,
And lights upon the poorest plot of all,
Where nought springs up but barren letter-thorns;
Say, how shall the poor poet his work begin?
He must, to bring you 'neath illusion's spell,
So interweave word-symbols that they paint
A picture, even such as Melos' own;
Yea, fortune favouring, even looks, sighs, and tears.

But vain the Sign's best effort if you fail
To rise therefrom to the intrinsic Real;
Tears in themselves are water, nothing more!
Therefore would you not your enjoyment mar,
Probe not too far the Sign's anatomy;
Embrace the Real that in the picture lives!—
Dead many of my pictures are, I know,—
Yet albeit few, I have some sparks of life;
Transcend me!—where I've smouldered, flash to fire!

Moreover, to conclude where I began,—
If you read poems, (for example mine)
Be willed, lives anything therein, to live it;
And just to live, for better cannot be,
Grasp or grasp not, the outward Sign, yet live it;
And seek not *that* Light which is born of evil!
Light, though't be visible, may not be grasped;
The words themselves of this concluding charge
Are dark to all who have not truly lived.—

---

[1] Homer is said by some to have been born at Melos.—*Trans.*

Thus much then for the many!—Those pure souls
For whom my song has sounded,—they know well
I have but borrowed fable's mask, that so
The hallow'd thing conceal'd therein may not
Blind suddenly *their* eyes who dimly see!—
For that, I've given the first book of the Valley,
Now, bold in God I dare announce the second;
But all for those alone whose insight knows
That Faith and Art and Yearning—these are LOVE.

Thou loving Brotherhood, I come to thee
One Easter-even, I and this my song!—
What though the world find foolishness in me,
(I'm right in one thing, if in much I'm wrong.)
Yet, least and last of all, myself I see,
And not for laurel crowns, but Light, I long!
O'er wounds, from wounds divine, streams radiance glorious;
Who there in love beholds it, stands victorious.

THE END.

www.ingramcontent.com/pod-product-compliance
Lightning Source LLC
Chambersburg PA
CBHW032131230426
43672CB00011B/2301